The Rarest and Most
Collectible Cars of the Performance Era

MILLION-DOLLAR
MUSCLE CARS

COLIN COMER
Photography by DAVID NEWHARDT

MOTORBOOKS

DEDICATION

This book is dedicated to enthusiasts of the last true era of collectible cars to ever leave Detroit: the 1964–1971 American Muscle Car.

First published in 2007 by Motorbooks, an imprint of MBI Publishing Company, Galtier Plaza, Suite 200, 380 Jackson Street, St. Paul, MN 55101 USA

Copyright © 2007 by Colin Comer and David Newhardt

All rights reserved. With the exception of quoting brief passages for the purposes of review, no part of this publication may be reproduced without prior written permission from the Publisher.

The information in this book is true and complete to the best of our knowledge. All recommendations are made without any guarantee on the part of the author or Publisher, who also disclaim any liability incurred in connection with the use of this data or specific details.

We recognize, further, that some words, model names, and designations mentioned herein are the property of the trademark holder. We use them for identification purposes only. This is not an official publication.

Motorbooks titles are also available at discounts in bulk quantity for industrial or sales-promotional use. For details write to Special Sales Manager at MBI Publishing Company, Galtier Plaza, Suite 200, 380 Jackson Street, St. Paul, MN 55101 USA

Editor: Darwin Holmstrom
Cover Design by: Michael Cawcutt
Designers: Sara Holle and James Kegley

Printed in Hong Kong

Library of Congress Cataloging-in-Publication Data

Comer, Colin.
  Million-dollar muscle cars : the rarest and most collectible cars of
the performance era / by Colin Comer ; photography by David Newhardt.
     p. cm.
  Includes index.
  ISBN-13: 978-0-7603-2952-8 (hardbound w/ jacket)
  ISBN-10: 0-7603-2952-4 (hardbound w/ jacket)
  1. Muscle cars--United States--History. 2. Muscle cars--Collectors
and collecting. I. Newhardt, David, 1955- II. Title.
  TL23.C63 2007
  629.222--dc22
                                          2007024583

On the cover:
The 1971 Hemi 'Cuda convertible that first broke the two-comma barrier.

On the frontispiece:
The console of Pete Estes' 1968 Z/28 convertible.

On the title pages:
The honk of the Hemi engine breathing through the Shaker hood scoop is clearly audible above the wind noise generated by the 'Cuda convertible at speed. Who needs a stereo when you can listen to music like that?

On the back cover:
Built for a Goodyear Tire test session, the 1967 Shelby GT500 Super Snake was one of the most powerful cars built in a decade defined by powerful cars.

CONTENTS

Introduction: Big-Money Muscle	6
Section 1: Million-Dollar Cars	10
Chapter One: 1970–1971 'Cuda & Challenger Hemi Convertibles	12
Chapter Two: 1965 Shelby GT350 R Models	28
Chapter Three: 1965 Hurst GeeTO Tiger	42
Chapter Four: 1967 Shelby GT500 Super Snake	56
Chapter Five: 1968 Camaro Z/28 Convertible	68
Chapter Six: 1969 Trans Am Convertibles	78
Chapter Seven: 1969 ZL1 Camaros	86
Chapter Eight: 1971 Sox & Martin Stock Hemi 'Cuda Car	96
Section 2: Six Figures and Rising	108
Chapter Nine: 1965 Hurst Motor Trend GTO Riverside 500 Pace Car	110
Chapter Ten: 1965–1966 Shelby GT350 Factory Drag Cars	120
Chapter Eleven: 1968 Mr. Norm's GSS 440 Dart	130
Chapter Twelve: 1969 Yenko 427 Nova	138
Chapter Thirteen: 1969 Dodge Charger Daytona Hemi	148
Chapter Fourteen: 1969–1971 Pontiac GTO Judge Round-Port Convertibles	158
Chapter Fifteen: 1970 Chevelle LS6 Convertible	172
Appendices	178
Appendix A: Alternatives to Million-Dollar Muscle	178
Appendix B: A Real-World Buyer's Guide	184
Index	190
Acknowledgments	192

INTRODUCTION

BIG-MONEY MUSCLE

Muscle cars were never intended to be valuable. In fact, the whole idea behind muscle cars was to make them inexpensive and fast. Muscle cars were stripped-down versions of the most utilitarian, homely, and basic mass-produced cars to ever roll out of Detroit. These rattle trap, bare bones, crude devices were built to conform to a price point with little regard given to sophistication or longevity, and aimed squarely at the youth market. And this market couldn't get enough of them. These were the cars every red-blooded American kid wanted. The image, the speed, the lifestyle were all highly addictive. Looking back, the muscle car years were a relatively brief moment in time that we will never see the likes of again. It was a perfect storm, just what the market wanted, and was presented at the right place in the right time.

So how did these seemingly disposable cars, built in large numbers and owned by kids who literally tried to kill them from the first twist of the key, become so valuable? More importantly, why did they become so valuable? Most people are astounded when they hear the recent sales results of the most desirable muscle cars. I call them the two-comma cars, cars that are worth so much money that you need two commas to separate all the zeroes in the price. To the uninitiated, a muscle car selling for over a million dollars is probably akin to catching the Loch Ness Monster on 10-pound test fishing line. That being said, out of the hundreds of

Previous page, main: One of the most successful 1965 Shelby GT350 R models of all time, 5R107.

Previous page, inset: Bookends meeting on a lonely desert road: the first and the last Hemi 'Cuda convertibles ever built are visually striking and brutally fast.

thousands of muscle cars, there are a handful of examples worthy of this price level. The ultra-rare. The mythical. The Loch Ness Monsters of the muscle car world.

The intent of this book is not to tell the story of the muscle car again, for it has been told many times before. If you know what leaded high-test smells like flowing through dual exhausts, you certainly don't need a refresher course. The goal here is to explore million-dollar muscle cars: to examine the actual cars that have been sold for this money, to get into the heads of the owners (past and present), and to learn why the sellers chose to sell and why the buyers stroked the checks with all those zeros. More importantly, I will dissect the cars and find just where the value lies, and what makes certain cars worth a million bucks or more. This is a rare glimpse into a world most will never see, an insider's look into a segment of the market that is often misunderstood, by cutting through the hype and made-for-television auction extravaganzas to find where the rubber really meets the road.

At this point, you may be curious as to my credentials and what makes me the right guy to write a book like this. How is it that a kid who didn't even grow up in the 1960s can write about cars that rolled off the assembly line before his time? I have always been fascinated by muscle cars and, from an early age, have researched and immersed myself in what I feel was the last era of truly collectible cars to ever be produced. I sought out people with incredible knowledge of these cars, and made myself their shadow. At 13 years old I was restoring GM muscle cars, and by 16 the freedom of a driver's license made it possible to do such things as crawl through junk yards collecting Pistol Grip shifters and Tri-Power induction setups. My best friends growing up were the guys twice my age with Six Pack Mopars and LS6 Chevelles. I have watched these cars go from socially unacceptable $1,500 beaters to being the most desirable collector cars on the market today. For the last 16 years I have built my collector car business into what many consider the premier high-end muscle car dealer in the country. I specialize in the ultra-rare, low-production cars that are the focus of this book. Who better to tell the story of high-end muscle cars than a guy who is involved in the market on a daily basis?

I not only sell the cars, but I have also been collecting them nearly my whole life. I often say that it is a shame many of today's buyers won't get to experience these cars the way we did when they were relatively inexpensive. Not many people will take their Hemi 'Cuda and drive it to the grocery store, or enter into an impromptu street battle. Now you have to worry about hurting an original engine or mortally wounding a nearly priceless collectible, which is a shame because using these cars is where the fun is. Living with a muscle car and learning its qualities (or lack thereof) are what endeared them to me and many others in the first place. On the other hand, the values being realized for the rarest and most significant muscle cars will preserve them for future generations, as well as save many from extinction. High values makes it sensible to rescue and properly restore rare cars, rather than let them rust into oblivion or be "restored" with cost being the main criteria, instead of making them correct and doing a proper restoration, which by definition entails bringing something back to new condition, flaws and all. An intimate knowledge of these cars gained through owning countless examples and using them as intended—whether it be racing or daily driver duties—as well as restoring, researching, and hunting them down for over two decades, has given me a unique perspective.

So why have muscle car values taken a virtual rocket ship ride to the moon? Looking at the collector car world as a whole, a few distinct themes are evident. Seasoned collectors will recite certain things that are the hallmarks of inherent value. A common thread is performance, regardless of the era you look at. And in the big picture, one can arguably break the most valuable collector cars down and place them in three distinct categories: prewar full classics, 1950s sports and racing cars, and American muscle cars. The one thing they all have in common is that they were ahead of their time in performance, whether it be a Duesenberg SJ, a pontoon-fendered 1958 Ferrari Testarossa, or a Super Duty Pontiac. These types of cars were limited-production, competition-proven cars in their day, and revolutionary at the time.

ZL1 Camaros are among the most valuable cars ever produced by General Motors' Chevrolet Division.

While muscle cars are a distinctly American phenomenon, those who think they do not have the same inherent Ferrari-like value gained through racing are sadly mistaken. In European road racing, only the ultra-wealthy independents or factory teams had the means to become truly successful. The average enthusiast was stuck on the sidelines watching and could never dream of being involved. But drag racing and factory-built muscle changed all of that. The average guy could go to a dealership and, armed with the right information, check all the right boxes, buy a car from the factory for not too much money, go racing, and win. The age-old saying of "win on Sunday, sell on Monday" is very true. Drag racing made competition attainable for the average guy and sold cars. Outside of drag racing, another American phenomenon was in place—National Association for Stock Car Auto Racing (NASCAR). The early days of stock car racing also fueled the fire for consumers wanting factory-built muscle.

What all this amounts to is the inherent core values for the most sought-after collectible cars are basically the same. They were all the best of their kind when new, all had an emphasis on performance, and all were proven in competition. Muscle cars resonate with many collectors because when they were new they were obtainable. An SJ Dusey was not an obtainable goal when new, nor were the best in 1950s road race cars or European marques. Add to this the fact that the average American kids wouldn't know what to do with a Ferrari if they had one, and the market was ready for a car they could relate to. A car they could use. A car that had performance in spades, was attainable, and wasn't intimidating. The muscle car era was the ultimate incarnation of these factors. And from this era, the ultra-rare, biggest, baddest, and most desirable cars when new are the most desirable cars of today. While not all of them are million-dollar muscle, the same qualities that define the few two-comma cars can be found in far less expensive cars. This is the beauty of the muscle car market. Just like when they were new, today an average guy can find the right car with the right ingredients and inherent value, and get involved.

What follows are examples of not only million-dollar muscle cars, but also less expensive ones that have the same qualities, as well as a careful evaluation of values. Is it a question of rarity, provenance, condition, or some magical combination? I invite you to strap in and get ready for a full-throttle blast through the quarter-mile as we search for the answer by looking at some of the most historically significant and, yes, the most valuable muscle cars of all time. ∎

SECTION 1
MILLION-DOLLAR CARS

CHAPTER ONE
1970–1971 PLYMOUTH HEMI 'CUDA CONVERTIBLES & 1970 DODGE CHALLENGER R/T HEMI CONVERTIBLES

Time is a funny thing. It makes us forget certain things and reflect on others through rose-colored glasses. Such is the case with the now legendary Mopar Hemi E Body convertibles. These are the undisputed kings of the two-comma muscle car record-holder club. Even people who drive Honda and Toyota hybrid cars know what a Hemi 'Cuda is, due to the unbelievable amount of press these cars have received as the top dogs of the collector car market in the last five years. But let's get back to that whole time thing. When these cars were new, nobody wanted them—well, almost nobody, to be more precise. Between both cars and both 1970 and 1971 model years, a grand total of 41 Hemi E Body convertibles were sold—worldwide. That's close enough to nobody wanting one in my book. After all, just like McDonald's cranking out burgers, if there were people in line with money, Chrysler would have kept taking their orders and turning out cars.

Why were these cars, now the 800-pound gorillas of the muscle car market, such slugs when new? From my perspective, there are a few key reasons. First, by 1970, its fourth year in production, the street Hemi had a bad reputation. What worked on the high banks of NASCAR at 7,000 rpm didn't work too well when dumbed down for street use. Hemis were tough to get tuned right and, once tuned, usually needed to be tuned again in short order. Much like Ford's Boss 429, sewer-sized ports with compromised intakes, a weak cam, and

Previous page, main: Fitting the fearsome Hemi engine into the new-for-1970 E-body resulted in an instant classic. Add the topless benefits of a convertible and the result would be legendary.

Previous page, inset: Race inspired hood pins flanked the huge hood, punctured by the functional shaker scoop. Few scoops were painted body color; most came in an accent color.

Top: Nicknamed the "Elephant," the 426-cubic-inch Hemi engine was developed for the track, yet succeeded on the street. Hemispherical combustion chamber design required a complex valve train arraignment that saw the spark plug sitting in the center of the combustion chamber.

Nail the throttle, and the sound of the air rushing into the functional shaker scoop of a 1971 Hemi 'Cuda is something not soon forgotten.

super-restrictive exhausts didn't help the mighty Hemi. Chrysler tried to make matters better in 1970 by fitting hydraulic lifters to eliminate valve adjustments, but they also served up valve float at the rpm these engines were designed to run. The bottom line was that a good running 440, especially the new-for-1969 440 Six Pack engine, would give a Hemi a real run for its money, and for about 600 bucks less.

Second, anybody in the market for a top-dog performance car really didn't want a heavy convertible. If you were paying all that money for an extra 35 horsepower, why strap on a few hundred more pounds in a less rigid chassis? Third, the E Body cars were—how should I say this—kind of crappy. They were rushed into production and, while beautifully styled, not exactly well engineered. Witness the doors that sound like a hardware store exploding when you shut them. The interiors were cheap, and the whole car had the typical Mopar cost-cutting feel about it. Everybody knew that while a 'Cuda or Challenger may handle OK on its torsion bar and leaf-spring suspension, neither rode all that well and both felt cheap. Add to this the fact that cutting the roof off of an E Body car made what was already a compromised chassis become a 425-horsepower toboggan, and you get a Hemi E Body convertible that was not what a serious speed freak wanted for street or drag racing.

I used to have a 440 Six Pack 'Cuda convertible about 10 years ago—a 4.10 geared, Torqueflite-equipped car. After launching the car hard a few times, for the next week the passenger's

14 ■ CHAPTER ONE

Per pony car design edict, long hood/short deck proportions defined the styling of the E-body. The diminutive trunk limited the amount of luggage that could be hauled, but with a Hemi under the hood, this car wasn't built to haul luggage.

door didn't really shut well and the crack at the top of the right quarter panel got pretty wide. And this was a nice, rust-free car.

Now, all the reasons not to want a car that you would have to live with on a daily basis really don't matter once the car becomes a collectible item. These cars do not get raced anymore and are rarely even driven. Thirty-seven years of knowledge gained through fixing and restoring E Bodies means that most of their factory sins can be corrected during restoration. And with a little care and massaging, even the street Hemis can be made to run like they should. The most positive result of Chrysler's fumbled attempt at marketing Hemi E Body convertibles is that they are among the rarest and most desirable muscle cars of all time. Think about it; they have the wildest and best-looking motor to ever leave Chrysler, in one of the best-looking cars ever, with tops that go down. They have the legend, they have the look, and they have the mystique. Best of all, they are among the rarest of all muscle cars, and that makes them the ultimate Mopar muscle car of all time.

Assembly line workers dreaded seeing the order for "billboard" side decals. Like most vehicles built during the 1970s, speed of assembly was paramount, not panel alignment. Workers tended to struggle to get the large decals aligned properly and without lots of air bubbles.

So let's get a handle on the value of these cars and the rocket ship ride it has been on for a few decades. Unwanted when new, within 10 years people started to seek out these special cars and pay a premium for them. By the late 1970s, they were roughly $10,000 cars. In the mid-1980s, they had gone to the mid $20,000 range. By the late 1980s, a good Hemi 'Cuda convertible sold just into six-figure territory. Another 10 years down the line, they were around a quarter of a million bucks. In December 1999, headline news was made when a 1971 Hemi 'Cuda convertible seized by police in a Washington State drug bust was sold at auction for $410,000. The local police department was thrilled, as the 'Cuda sale paid for a fleet of new squad cars! By 2001–2002, Hemi convertibles became serious commodities, with a few 1971 'Cuda convertibles changing hands in the $500,000–$750,000 range.

Then something happened that really pulled the pin. In late 2002, collector Milton Robson of Atlanta placed a half-page ad in *Hemmings Motor News* for his one-of-two 1971 Hemi 'Cuda four-speed convertible, a car he had owned since 1988. Milton had a few lines about the car, with the price in big, bold type for all to see: $1,000,000. For a Mopar. Oh boy, I thought, dogs and cats are sleeping together and the sky is falling! I immediately called my friend Dana Mecum, president of Mecum

Auctions, to tell him about Milton's ad. When he picked up the phone, before I had a chance to say anything, Dana said, "Did you see Milton's ad in *Hemmings*?"

The game was on; muscle cars were into two-comma dough. While these cars had been trading for money close to Milton's $1 million price, they were all private sales and not public knowledge. But this ad in the bible of the hobby changed all that. Milton sold his car for $1,000,000 to an infamous broker known as much for his shady dealings and big mouth as anything else. But the word was out that the car sold. Soon, the broker had the car on eBay, reporting it sold for $1.3 million. The deal didn't materialize, and the car bounced around a little before ending up with a well-known Mopar collector in Illinois. In September 2003, CNN published an article on million-dollar muscle cars being a reality. On the cover of the December 2003 *Mopar Action* magazine, Milton's old car was featured with the headline "$1,000,000 'Cuda—The Inside Story." Big-dollar muscle was now headline news. Robson's old blue car has moved around a few times since, most recently trading hands at auction in January 2007 for $2,420,000.

Once the ball was rolling, Hemi 'Cuda convertible prices took off running. While every sales result since the late 1970s had doubled the prior one, by now these cars were at such substantial dollar

When the 1970 Hemi 'Cuda debuted, an optional and subtle "hockey stripe" tape graphic adorned the side. But the '71 version went for a splashier statement with its optional and aptly named "billboard" decals.

Like most pony cars, the Hemi 'Cuda used a 2+2 seating configuration. While the back seat occupants might struggle for legroom, they couldn't complain when the driver flat footed the throttle.

amounts that this doubling was serious. Wild reports of multi-million-dollar sales became the norm. Twelve months after its last million-dollar headline, in December 2004, *Mopar Action* featured a white 1971 Hemi 'Cuda convertible on its cover with the headline: "World's Most Valuable Muscle Car! $2 Million Hemi 'Cuda." The feature car was the last Hemi 'Cuda convertible built and one of the two export models produced, having been originally sold in France. It had recently been passed through the hands of a few well-known Mopar collectors, the last being Carlos Monteverde of Kensington, England, who had recently sold it to noted Hemi ragtop collector Bill Weimann of Arizona. In September 2005, Weimann reportedly turned down a $4.1 million bid for this car at the Rand/Workman auction in New York. Another sale of a 1971 'Cuda convertible was reported in 2005 at $3 million. In January 2006, collector Dave Christenholz of Arizona sold his 1970 Hemi 'Cuda convertible at the Barrett-Jackson auction for $2,160,000. As 1970 Hemi 'Cudas have always traded for perhaps 30–40 percent less than 1971 model year versions, this result was spot-on. The buyer was none other than Bill Weimann, who at this point owned three other Hemi 'Cuda convertibles. Numerous news reports of these sales and related values have been published, seeing print in such mainstream publications as the *New York Times,* and *USA Today*.

Anyone foolish enough to challenge a 1971 Hemi 'Cuda to a street race was living in a fantasy world.

In a strange twist of fate, Hemi 'Cuda convertibles went full circle from being a little-wanted curiosity when new to becoming the poster child and barometer for an entire market almost 40 years later. Who would have guessed it?

The Curious Yellow 1971 Hemi 'Cuda convertible on these pages is perhaps the most famous Hemi E Body in existence. It was sold new to its original owner at Kennedy Chrysler-Plymouth in Milwaukee, Wisconsin. It is the only Curious Yellow 'Cuda convertible built and is a well-equipped car with a Torqueflite automatic, white interior, and many options. The original owner sold the car, and after a few interim owners, it ended up in Madison, Wisconsin, in 1986, where it was owned by Bill Stickman. In the fall of 1985, Stickman advertised the car in *Hemmings Motor News* for $24,000. Steve Segal of Connecticut saw the ad, immediately phoned Stickman, and secured the deal with a deposit. Segal drove to Wisconsin with an open car trailer hooked to his K5 Blazer and loaded up the 'Cuda along with a truckload of new old stock (NOS) parts included with which to restore the car. Surviving a terrible winter storm, the 'Cuda made it home with Segal, who restored it over the next few months. Ready in time for the 1986 Muscle Car Nationals, Segal took the car to the event to show it off and do a little drag racing. Segal recalls the car was a slug; its best time in the quarter-mile

The E-body design was admired for its taut lines and subtle surface tension. The power of the Hemi engine wasn't quite so subtle.

was a 14.50 at 99 miles per hour. When he was beat by a four-door Chevy Caprice with a 427, the nails were in the 'Cuda's coffin—it was an embarrassment.

In March 1987, Segal was contacted by Greg Joseph on behalf of legendary collector Otis Chandler. They were on a mission to build the best muscle car collection in existence and decided they needed to buy the crown jewel first. Once the word got out that Chandler was buying muscle cars, the fear was that prices would go crazy. Segal told them he wanted $54,000 for the yellow 'Cuda, and they immediately purchased it. Since this sale, Segal has been accused more than once of "ruining" the market for enthusiasts by sending Hemi prices into orbit. After eight years in Chandler's collection, the 'Cuda was sold to collector Kevin Suydam of Seattle, Washington, for a reported $250,000. Suydam sold the car to Dave Christenholz in 2001 for $775,000, and then purchased the one-of-two 1971 'Cuda four-speed convertibles built, the same car that sold for $410,000 in 1999. The Curious Yellow 'Cuda is the car that actor Don Johnson saw in a muscle car book in 1995. He

Unlike many big-block engines that generated the bulk of their power at low- and midlevel rpm's, the race-bred Hemi lived to spin at high rpm's.

Dodge fitted a special decal under the hood of vehicles equipped with the optional Shaker hood. The huge air cleaner/scoop assembly pretty much covered the top of the engine. Adjusting your dual quads now took an extra 30 minutes!

As 1971 wound to a close, so did the career of the 426-cubic-inch Hemi. Certifying the huge engine for increasingly stringent emission regulations would prove financially unsound for Chrysler due to the low number of Hemis sold.

Right: Plymouth installed front fender vents on the 'Cuda for just one year: 1971. This was an era when manufacturers made notable styling changes each year to keep a model line fresh and different from preceding years.

later had copies of the 'Cuda made for him to use on his TV show *Nash Bridges*. The original has been featured in numerous books, magazines, and other publications for the over 20 years. What's it worth? Well, if history repeats itself as it has, about twice what it sold for the last time.

The other car featured is also from Dave Christenholz's collection of rare muscle cars. It is a 1970 Dodge Challenger R/T Hemi convertible, one of five four-speed cars produced and one of twelve Hemi convertibles total. With a Plum Crazy Hi-Impact paint applied to the car, it is the quintessential Challenger R/T. Hemi Challenger convertibles, although considered "upscale" cars from the 'Cudas when new, have always traded for roughly half of comparable Hemi 'Cuda convertibles in the marketplace. As an example, in 2003, when 1971 Hemi 'Cuda convertibles were selling for $1 million,

One of the most powerful attractions of a muscle car is its aggressive stance, shown to good effect with the 1971 Hemi 'Cuda. Period Polyglas tires, looking ridiculously narrow by contemporary standards, were state of the art performance shoes in 1971.

a Hemi Challenger convertible sold for $450,000. They were built only for the 1970 model year, and none of the 12 came with a Shaker hood; it was an available option that none of the 12 buyers opted to order.

This example was rescued in 2004 after years of being disassembled and locked away by a previous owner. Christenholz sent the car, in pieces, to the award-winning Mopar restoration experts at Aloha Dream Cars in Port Washington, Wisconsin. Still fitted with its original numbers-matching drivetrain, it emerged from restoration in 2005 looking even better than it could have on the showroom floor in 1970. If there is a value buy in the Hemi E Body market, it would be a Challenger. One-year production versus two, 12 built versus 30, and all the same stuff under the skin. Perhaps because they so rarely change hands, the Challenger market has not been able to establish itself in a public forum, thereby keeping the values down. Whatever the case, to buy a car similar to the purple one on these pages, figure on right around a million bucks—this is an exclusive club to get into.

So where are the values heading? Logic would tell us that the unprecedented appreciation in such a short time is not sustainable with these cars. As deep into the two-comma money as these cars are, there is a limited pool of buyers. As with anything, supply and demand will dictate values, and right now perhaps every wealthy collector that desires a Hemi E Body convertible has one. If another one hits the market soon, and the cast of characters that have been buying these cars does not get involved, the muscle cars could quickly have a price adjustment. However, if the current owners hold their cars for years, as has happened with many of them in the past, the next buyer that comes along looking for a Hemi E Body convert will have to raise the bar again to shake one loose. Only time, the owners, and the prospective buyers will set the stage for what comes next. Regardless of what happens, it is guaranteed to be as exciting to watch as it has been for the last 20 years. ∎

By definition, a muscle car is a huge engine stuffed into an intermediate body, and the 1971 Hemi 'Cuda followed that formula to the letter.

Even though fewer Challenger convertibles received Hemi engines than did convertible 'Cudas—12 versus 30—historically the Challengers have commanded roughly half the price of comparable 'Cudas. But because these cars are so rare and change hands so infrequently, it is hard to put a definitive value on them.

CHAPTER TWO

1965 SHELBY GT350 FACTORY COMPETITION MODELS

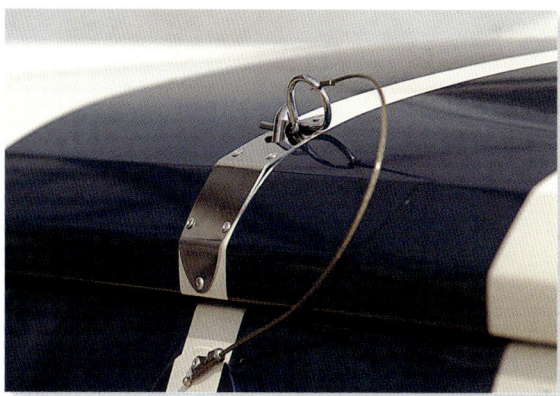

In 1964, Ford introduced its new Mustang. While based on the pedestrian Falcon chassis, the Mustang's new long hood/short deck design was a hit and the first of what we now call "pony cars." Ford put the hurt on GM and Chrysler with the Mustang, and as the competition scrambled to come up with something to compete with it, Ford was selling every Mustang it could build as fast as it could get them to dealers. However, even with this jump on the competition, Ford knew it would take more to sell Mustangs after the novelty wore off. If any company knew that performance sold cars, it was Ford.

The Mustang was a decent car, but certainly not a muscle car and in no way a sports car. It was a compact that was quickly earning a reputation as a "secretary's car," not as a performance car. Knowing that the Mustang was never going to be a hit with the same buyers who went for the Pontiac GTO or similar GM intermediates, Ford took aim at the sports car crowd. When a bid to get the Sports Car Club of America (SCCA) to accept the Mustang for competition was denied, Ford didn't quit but rather looked for another angle. That angle was Texan Carroll Shelby, the same guy Ford was supplying with engines for his Cobra. Shelby's Cobra sports car was putting the racing world, including the SCCA, on its ear. Shelby clearly knew how to make the Ford 289 work. Ford figured if Shelby's crew of engineers could make that old oxcart, buggy-spring equipped AC sports car win

Previous page, main: Only 36 R Models were built, none for use on public streets. They were available in any color as long as it was Wimbledon White with blue stripes.

Previous page, inset: Quick access to the trunk was required, as the fuel filler was hidden in the trunk. To help gain fast entry, a lanyard-mounted pin was used, and once you were in there, a large quick-fill cap and built-in funnel aided in fast refueling.

The R Model's race-prepared 289-cubic-inch engine generated over 350 horsepower. The "Monte Carlo" bar connecting the top of the shock towers helped to reduce front-end flex under hard cornering.

races, surely they could make the Mustang into a competitive mount. "Cute" sells cars for a while, but winning races and having a performance image sells cars indefinitely.

To give the Mustang teeth enough to bite into the performance market, Ford needed not only to race, but to win. The SCCA mandated that for Shelby's Cobra Mustang to be accepted, it had to meet a few requirements. There had to be at least 100 street and competition versions produced; they had to be two-seaters; and the competition version could have a modified suspension *or* engine from the street version, but not both. Shelby wisely decided to develop the suspension and produce both street and competition versions with the same setup. Building the cars with a hot "race" motor for street use would render them nearly useless. A competition suspension, on the other hand, was just fine for street use and actually quite desirable for Shelby's intended market.

After much development, the new Shelby Mustang made a heck of a competition car, in spite of its very humble beginnings. With relatively simple modifications by Shelby's skilled engineers and mechanics, the GT350 Competition Model, or R Model as it has come to be known, became nearly unbeatable in B/Production competition. Basic weight-cutting procedures such as eliminating bumpers and using Plexiglas windows, a fiberglass front apron and hood, and a gutted interior made the competition version GT350 a fit and trim race car. This, combined with 289-ci K Code engines, which took advantage of Shelby's three years of experience using the same motor in the Cobra competition cars, resulted in a formula still in use with countless vintage racers today. To list all of the races won by GT350 R Models would take up this entire book. It will have to suffice to say that I do not believe there has been another production-based car built in such small numbers to have won so many races. The Shelby GT350 R literally took the racing world by storm—just as Ford had hoped and intended. In 1965, GT350 R Models won five out of six regional SCCA championships. At the 1965 American Road Race of Champions (ARRC) national race, 10 out of the 14 B/Production cars entered were R Models. By the end of the race, Jerry Titus had won the 1965 B/Production National Championship in 5R001. The Mustang now not only had teeth, but it also had fangs.

30 ■ CHAPTER TWO

Of the three body styles that the Mustang was offered in, the fastback had the best aerodynamic characteristics; thus, Shelby picked it as the basis for his race-only model.

Right: In an effort to reduce weight and reduce drag, the B-pillar vents were replaced with a piece of aluminum pop riveted to the body.

A total of 36 R Model cars were built in three batches. Two cars were considered prototypes, and 34 were production models built for customers. The production versions were priced at $5,995, about $1,500 more than a street version GT350. A quick lesson in 1965 Shelby serial numbers: all start with "SFM" for *Shelby Ford Mustang*, followed by the number "5" for the model year *1965*, followed by (after car No. 31) either the letter "S" for *street* or "R" for *race*, followed by the sequential production number. There were 562 cars of all varieties built, so the sequential production numbers range from 001 to 562.

The first of the initial 15 customer R Models was SFM5R094, delivered on April 10, 1965, to Tom Yeager of Marion, Ohio. The last first-batch car, SFM5R108, was delivered on September 22,

The R Model front apron was built of fiberglass. It may seem strange for a race car, but the turn signals were functional. This is a very popular look, and many street Mustangs and Shelbys have been retrofitted with an R Model valance over the years.

Because of the high speeds that the R Model generated, a vent had to be molded at the top of the Plexiglas rear window to keep it from popping out of the frame due to increased cabin air pressure.

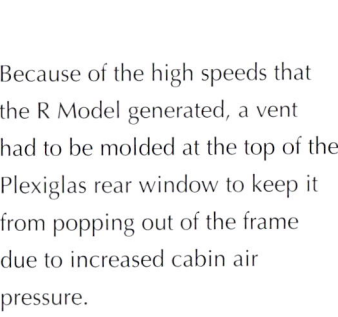

1965, to Gene Hammond Ford in Texas and sold to its first owner Bill Steele.

One of these first-batch cars is featured here. It is SFM5R107, which possesses one of the most impressive R Model race histories. As one of only three first-batch cars to be shipped outside of the United States when new, R107 is one of the R Models responsible for putting the rest of the world on notice that there was a new sheriff in town. R107 was purchased new by Ford Advanced Vehicles (FAV) in England on September 7, 1965. It was then delivered to its first owner, ex–Cobra factory team driver Jochen Neerpasch of Germany. Neerpasch was racing at the time for the legendary Alan Mann Racing Team in Germany, driving a Mustang coupe. Neerpasch decided to form his own team with another successful European touring car driver, Freiherr von Wendt, using R107. Freiherr von Wendt raced R107 in the Nurburgring 1000 race in 1966 and, in spite of almost complete transmission failure leaving him with only fourth gear, he won the GT class. Neerpasch then took R107 to a race at Hockenheim, and once again R107 won the GT class, this time with the help of all four forward ratios in the transmission. This success was followed by another notable GT class win by von Wendt at Nurnberg with a second place win overall for the event.

On November 26, 1966, after winning some very significant events with R107, Neerpasch advertised R107 for sale in the *Auto Motor Sport* newspaper. Friedhelm Theissen purchased R107 on April 18, 1967, immediately sending the engine to John Wyer of J. W. Automotive. Wyer was Ford's European GT40 team manager and an important part of Ford's victory at Le Mans. He was the right

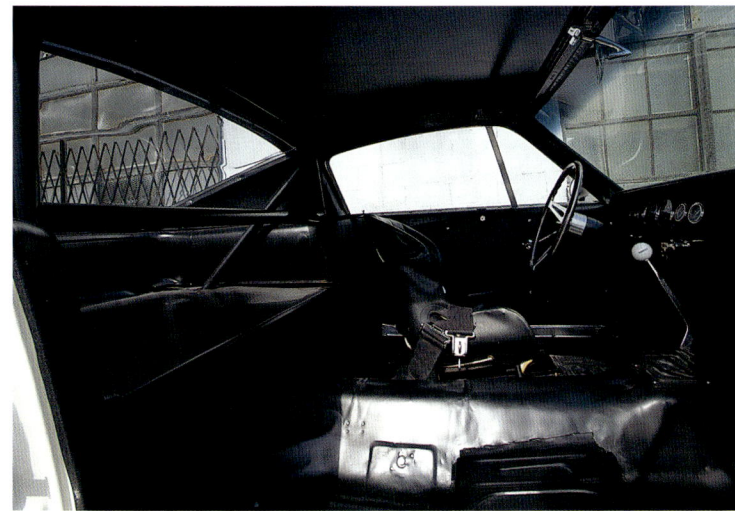

guy to put R107 into shape for further victories. Theissen entered R107 in the European equivalent of the U.S. Trans-Am series, the Deutsche Rundsheckenmeisterschaft. In over eight races, Theissen never finished lower than second place. This put Theissen and R107 first in GT and third overall for the entire series in 1967! Remember, this was a two-year-old race car taking on the best Europe had to offer on tracks much better suited for long-legged European sports cars than brutish American GT cars.

A picture of R107 racing at Nurburgring was featured on the cover of *Rallye Racing* magazine in July 1967. R107 was clearly making an impact in Europe. As time went on, R107 continued to race and win throughout Europe with different owners and drivers. In 1968, right after Hans Braun purchased the R107, he decided he wanted to try out his new race car. Braun was not a race driver but, in fact, was a car dealer. Undeterred, Braun purchased a touring pass to run R107 at Nurburgring. On a particularly tricky section, the helmetless Braun lost control of R107 and took a trip through the woods, damaging the right front fender and door of R107, along with his head (the lack of a helmet suggests it may have been empty anyway). Braun never drove the car again and sold it to Martin Rath, also a car dealer in Germany.

Rath was not a particularly honest sort, and along with stealing cars and shipping them to Saudi Arabia, he also hatched a plan to make money with R107. Rath would paint and letter R107 in a prospective sponsor's livery, present a plan for sponsorship, and get a deposit from the sponsor toward a season's sponsorship fee. Once this was accomplished, R107 would be painted in another prospective sponsor's livery and another deposit would be obtained. Rinse, lather, repeat! After doing this to a number of sponsors, Rath fled the country. While all of this was going on, Rath's driver, Walter Buhl, was racing R107 and winning over 20 races from 1968 to 1970. Buhl sold R107 in March 1970.

Passing through more owners, R107 continued to be raced very successfully throughout Europe. It was raced not only in Germany, but also in the Netherlands, Italy, Austria, and even Czechoslovaka. In 1973, the Oberste Nationale Sportbehörde (similar to the SCCA) told R107's owner that it was too old to continue racing. Refusing to give up, he installed 1968 Mustang front

The rulebook allowed R Models to race without a rear bumper; in the pursuit of weight savings, it was sent to the dumpster.

Left: Shelby advertised that the interior of the R Model was fire retardant, another term for gutted. A roll bar was installed, while pretty much everything else was yanked out. Light equals fast.

R Models were basic racing machines. A full slate of instruments monitored engine conditions, while the aluminum T-10M's shifter kept the right hand busy. Deep bolsters on the driver's seat worked with the racing seat belts to keep the driver on the left side of the interior. Proving that people were smaller 40 years ago, the R Model driver's seat is a tight fit for all but the most petite race jockeys.

Regulations stated that the dashboard of the stock car must be used, but there was nothing said about filling it with aftermarket gauges. Note the use of the stock switchgear.

fenders, grille, and valance, repainted the car, and presented it as a "1969 Shelby." R107 was issued a new log book and continued to race in disguise through 1978. In 1980, then owner Walter Hesterman parked R107 behind the service station he owned just outside of Frankfurt, Germany. R107 was just another old race car, far beyond its useful life and a difficult car to restore in Germany. In 1984, a German SAAC (Shelby American Automobile Club) member found R107 and contacted SAAC headquarters in the United States. Word spread, and Bob Cote purchased R107 from Hesterman on February 10, 1986, for the whopping sum of 1,000 DM, or about US$500. Before R107 left Germany, it was sold to Craig Conley of California. Conley, a highly knowledgeable Shelby enthusiast, traveled to Germany and spent almost two months visiting past owners and drivers of R107, collecting information, trophies, and pictures. Upon his return to the States, Conley began the restoration of R107. In 2006, Conley sold R107 to Paul Pfugfelder before the restoration was completed. Pfugfelder sent the car to noted R Model specialist Curt Vogt at Cobra Automotive in Wallingford, Connecticut, for completion. Restored to its original 1965 specification, R107 made its debut at the 2006 SAAC National Convention at Virginia International Raceway. It has since been sold to Ron Krolick of New York.

After the first batch was completed, the second batch of R Models was produced. The chassis numbers for these cars went from 5R209 to 5R213, for a total of five cars. The third and final batch of R Models consisted of 14 cars, all but one being delivered post-January 1966. As they were built so

Freiherr von Wendt pilots 5R107 to victory in the Nurburgring 1000 at Germany's famed Nurburgring in 1966. *Colin Comer Collection*

late in the 1965 model year, the third-batch cars actually had 1966 GT350 grilles and tape rocker panel stripes. By this point, R Model buyers were drying up, as $6,000 would get them any number of new race cars. Evidence of this is shown with the second car featured here—the last R Model to be sold from Shelby American, 5R533, shipped on March 31, 1967.

The 5R533 was delivered to Fogg Motors Ltd. of Westminster, British Colombia, through Ford of Canada. Fogg Motors sold it to Brown Brothers Ford of Vancouver, British Columbia. Brown Brothers put Canadian hot-shoe Tommy Hamilton of Campbell River, British Columbia, in the driver's seat of 5R533. Hamilton, a quite accomplished privateer racer, had won 38 of 54 races entered in a variety of sports cars prior to signing on with Brown Brothers. Hamilton, used to making do with underpowered British sports cars, was now a true force to be reckoned with in R533. With Hamilton at the wheel, the Brown Brothers R533 was to become what has been called by SAAC R Model Registrar Howard Pardee the "winningest GT350 R Model of all time."

Hamilton had a unique, Smokey Yunick–like view of the rule book for production sports car racing in Canada. Hamilton loved to race, and to race as much as possible, Hamilton would change R533 to conform to many different racing classes. This was done by changing wheel and tire combinations, induction systems, and carburetion. By doing this, R533 could be raced by Hamilton in not only B/Production, but also A/Production-Modified, B/Production-Improved, C/Production-Modified, Improved Production, and the Over 2-liter Sports Racing groups. On top of this, Hamilton had enough guts to even enter R533 in assorted Pro races with Can-Am cars! The R533 and Hamilton racked up over 40 wins in two years of racing. During 1967, one notable finish for R533 was the Westwood Pro Invitational where Hamilton placed seventh overall in R533—the top six finishers were Can-Am cars. Not bad for a three-year-old Mustang. In 1968, Hamilton won no less than five national championships driving R533. To list the races won by Hamilton in R533, or even just to list the number of articles published in the period of his races in R533, would take a full page.

By 1969, Hamilton decided to go stock car racing; for a 40-year-old family man, stock car racing paid better and kept him closer to home. Brown Brothers offered Hamilton R533 for $1,800, but nothing is older than last year's race car. A stock car racer sure didn't need a well-used production sports racing car. Brown Brothers placed an ad for the R533 in *Motorsport* magazine's April 1970:

> FOR SALE: READY TO RACE—SHELBY COBRA. '66 Award winning Shelby Mustang runs in A Modified "B" improved production. Has won 28 of 33 races entered last year. Company policy dictates sale because of withdrawal from racing. $2800.00. Contact: F. Barter, Gen. Sales Manager. Brown Bros. Motors.

By 1972, R533 found a new home with Jeff Smith of Canada, who sold it to Mike Stidwell of Vancouver, British Columbia, in 1975. Stidwell began restoring R533 to 1966 specs, but in 1984, before the restoration was completed, he sold the car to William Roush of Washington. Roush completed the restoration and vintage-raced R533 until 1987, when he sold it to George Watters of California. R533 then passed through a quick succession of owners, including SAAC National Director Ken Eber.

R533 won a different kind of competition at the SAAC National Convention in 1991 when it won a first place in the concours car show. Apparently being a show pony did not suit R533, as its next owner, Peter Rogal of Boston, sent it to Cobra Automotive to be race-prepped so R533 could again return to the track. R533 was vintage-raced extensively through 2005, including a reunion with its first driver, Tommy Hamilton, at the SAAC National Convention in California in 2005. Hamilton, allowed by R533's owner and SAAC officials, was given the track at Fontana for a few "parade laps." Thirty-six years had passed since the last time Hamilton had twisted R533's ignition key, but after getting his old friend up to temperature, he shocked spectators and track officials alike when the 70-something Hamilton came screaming down the front straight in R533 at over 165 miles per hour! Immediately flagged in, and almost ejected from the event, Hamilton to this day is asking how to get started in vintage racing. In 2006, R533 was again sold. The current owner, acutely aware that a piece of history like R533 should not be raced competitively anymore, returned the car to Cobra Automotive again to be returned to proper 1965 R Model specifications. Today, R533 sits exactly as it did the first day Tommy Hamilton strapped in and entered his first race for Brown Brothers Ford, Vancouver, British Columbia.

1965 SHELBY GT350 FACTORY COMPETITION MODELS

Previous page: Body modifications were held to a minimum on all 36 R Models due to regulations. In an effort to save weight, the stock glass door and vent windows were replaced with Plexiglas windows, riding in aluminum frames and operated with cloth straps.

Twin hood pins held the fiberglass hood in place, while the functional scoop fed the engine compartment cool ambient air.

In yet another simple yet effective move, the exhaust pipes exited in front of the rear tires. By reducing the length of exhaust pipe, another few horsepower were extracted, and the exhaust could be dropped quickly for undercarriage access.

So where do 1965 Shelby GT350 R Models fit into the big picture? Whereas the Shelby Cobra established Shelby as a builder of world-beating sports cars, the original GT350 R Models did even more than that. By taking the somewhat vanilla Mustang and putting it on the performance map, the 36 R Models produced are a very significant part of Mustang and Shelby history. Had the 1965 GT350 been a failure, Shelby likely would have faded into history as the man who built the world champion Cobra and helped Ford defeat Ferrari at Le Mans. These accomplishments are not to be taken lightly by any stretch of the imagination, but think of what the success of the first Shelby Mustangs in competition did. They established Shelby as a manufacturer on a large scale, and Shelby Mustangs were produced in reasonably large numbers until 1970. Today, anything with the Shelby name on it is a guaranteed hit—witness the new 2007 GT500 and Shelby GTs being sold by Ford. It is reasonable to attribute a great deal of this fame to the 1965 R Model cars. These 36 cars, mostly campaigned by private race teams, were so good, so reliable, and had such phenomenal support from Shelby that they made an impact few cars have or will ever be able to duplicate.

The significance of the R Models was recognized by collectors very early on. Just as the cars became moderately competitive "old race cars" in the early 1970s, people realized they were special and started collecting them. Today, 30 of the 34 original R Models are accounted for, over 88 percent of the original production run. Value? R Models have historically sold for roughly three times what a good street GT350 has. Currently, good street 1965 GT350s are selling for roughly $300,000. Of

Tommy Hamilton took home five different West Coast championships in a 5R533, and in the process, the car came through virtually unscathed, an exceptionally rare occurrence in racing. Few R Models have survived as intact as the ones on these pages.

course, there are good R Models and bad ones; as with any race car, history and originality are key. Not many R Models escaped without serious on-track incidents, and finding one with great race history and most of its original DNA intact is a challenge. Re-bodies and substantial repairs were not frowned upon when these were old race cars, but as collectible items potential buyers need to do their homework. Good R Models have sold for impressive amounts. R102 sold at auction in 2006 for $990,000, yet the R108, needing restoration, sold for $750,000, also at the auction, in the same year. Should one of the factory engineering or team cars, the Titus 1965 B/Production champion R001 or the Ken Miles car R002 (the first R Model built), ever come up for sale, I would expect a value of at least twice any other R Model. These cars have unquestioned historical significance, double-digit production numbers, and appeal to not only muscle car but also sports car buyers. Just like famous prewar Grand Prix cars, Shelby GT350 R Models have the right credentials to be among the most sought-after collectible performance cars for decades to come. ∎

Before this Jochen Neerpasch–driven R Model 5R107 hit the racetrack, it was modified by John Wyer of Ford Advanced Vehicles in Slough/Bucks UK.

The battery was mounted in the trunk on the passenger side in an attempt to counter the driver's weight. Shelby made up the R Model's fuel tank by slicing two Mustang fuel tanks in half and welding the bottom sections together.

Right: One of the few body modifications made on R Models was the gentle rolling out of the wheel arches to make room for racing tires.

Top: What looks like a huge funnel actually directs air into the voracious 780-cfm Holley 4-barrel carburetor. Each valve cover utilized a raised breather to prevent pressure build-up. The tall vent tubes prevented oil from coming through the breathers and hitting the hot exhaust, where it could ignite.

CHAPTER THREE

THE 1965 HURST GeeTO TIGER

If one considers real muscle cars to be the classic "ten pounds of motor in a five pound bag," then the 1964 GTO was indeed the first real muscle car. This debate has been raging for years, with everything from Twin-H powered Hudson Hornets to Chrysler 300 letter cars being credited as the first muscle car. There is no debate, however, that the GTO was the first intermediate car to be stuffed with a full-size car engine and that it marked the beginning of the era this book is about.

In 1965—the GTO's sophomore model year—marketing guru and godfather of the GTO, Jim Wangers, along with Pontiac, George Hurst, and Petersen Publishing, put together a special contest to promote the GTO and Hurst Performance Products. The contest was based on a special album recorded by the Tigers on the Colpix label, entitled *GeeTO TIGER*. The flip side was the "Big Sounds of the GeeTO TIGER," which was reported to be recorded at speed on the GM test track, including wide-open acceleration, high-speed cornering, brake testing, and the like. In reality, the "test track" recordings were a studio creation, much like the Tigers themselves. Ah, the innocence of the 1960s.

In 1965, Pontiac was still trying to hook people on a hip nickname for the GTO, and "gee-toe" was one the company thought would work. Of course, it never

Previous page, main: The 1965 Hurst GeeTO Tiger was a contest car. To win the car, contestants had to correctly count how many times the word "Tiger" was mentioned in the "GeeTO Tiger" song and explain in 25 words or less why they deserved to win. The correct number was 42.

Previous page, inset: A 389-cubic-inch V-8 sits beneath the Hurst GeeTO's hood. With a Tri-Power carburetor setup, it was rated at 360 horsepower. Also fitted is the ultra rare factory Transistorized Ignition.

A big engine in an intermediate platform was the formula for the original muscle car, a formula produced by the original GTO. With help from George Hurst and Jim Wangers, the Hurst GeeTO Tiger was a high-exposure vehicle that garnered a lot of attention.

caught on; as is the case with many things, the public will arrive at its own nicknames rather than one being force-fed to it. As we know now, the one that stuck for the GTO was "Goat." Go figure.

The grand prize for the Pontiac/Hurst contest was a 1965 GTO named the "GeeTO Tiger." Specially equipped with over 28 factory options, plus special gold Hurst mag wheels, a special Hurst Gold paint job, and a gold-plated Hurst shifter, it was the ultimate 1965 GTO—and the ultimate promotional vehicle for all involved. Jim Wangers recalled the car in an interview that appeared in the January 1983 issue of *Classic Sixties*:

> The top prize . . . was this very special GTO, [the] GeeTO TIGER, which was built by Hurst. They actually sponsored the promotion with a lot of cooperation from Pontiac. It was done in a very special paint—what they called Hurst Gold in those days—which we renamed Tiger Gold. It was a Tri-Power, 4-speed with all the good stuff—Safe-T-Track, close ratio 4-speed, and suspension package. It was a Tiger Gold car with a black vinyl top, which in those days was very in. . . . It had a very special set of gold Hurst wheels and it had [Uniroyal Tiger Paw] redline tires—and this was used as a dual promotion to promote not only the record, but obviously the GTO—and Hurst, which was a very important part of Pontiac promotion as we were the first car [company] to ever put a Hurst shifter in right from the factory. [The contest car] had a lot of luxury options. It was not a race car per se; it was a nice total street machine. It had power steering, power brakes, because it was supposed to

be the nicest GTO you could put your hands on. It was a special car put together just for that program. It came through as a regular car and it was promoted as being a Royal Bobcat. The Hurst conversion was done locally—Hurst had a big shop here. Hurst Gold—actually, a derivative of Hurst Gold in '65—became a regular production option in 1966. It was a big seller in '66—it was called Tiger Gold by Pontiac both for the GTO and LeMans. In fact, we introduced the '67 Firebird in that color.

The GeeTO Tiger was heavily promoted in every automotive magazine for months in 1965, with full-page ads and lots of editorial coverage. Both Hurst and Pontiac advertised the car. Pontiac featured the record in many of its ads, and in total, over 450,000 *GeeTO TIGER* albums were distributed. These albums are highly sought after by collectors today, and there were three versions released. Some had a flip side of "The GeeTO PROWL" in place of the "Big Sounds of the GeeTO TIGER." All promotional versions had a record sleeve or an insert with instructions on how to enter the "Win a Tiger!" contest, and the prizes were listed, with the grand prize being the original GeeTo Tiger, second and third prizes being a complete set of Hurst mag wheels, fourth and fifth–place prizes new Hurst four-speed floor shifters, sixth and seventh Hurst three-speed floor shifters, and eighth through tenth–place winners receiving an Auto-Stereo unit, installed with 15 preselected tape cartridges. Ninety more winners were selected, winning everything from Colpix albums to magazine subscriptions from Petersen.

George Hurst's favorite color was a shade of gold he dubbed Hurst Gold. When applied to a 1965 GTO, it gave the contest car serious flash. George Hurst loved flash!

Gold-plated wheels wouldn't work on any other car but the 1965 Hurst GeeTO Tiger. With the exception of a nearly 30-year-old repaint and an engine rebuild, the car is all original.

Stacked headlights were seeing their first year of use when the 1965 Hurst GeeTO Tiger hit the circuit. The light configuration helped to emphasize the Wide Track Pontiac style of the 1960s.

Obviously, what every entrant wanted was the grand prize: "A 1965 G.T.O 'GeeTO TIGER' Hardtop; with all performance options added, including Hurst accessories and Tigerized interior!"

To win the contest, you had to listen to the song "GeeTO Tiger" and count the number of times the word "tiger" was sung. You were then instructed to submit this number along with a 25-word or less paragraph to be entitled, "Why I'd like to win the Original GeeTO TIGER," along with your name and address. The deadline was midnight, July 31, 1965. Do you think anyone from Hurst was waiting by the company's mailbox at 11:59 p.m.? Probably not. On July 27, 1965, after seeing an ad for the contest in *Hot Rod* magazine, Alex Lampone, a 19-year-old from West Allis, Wisconsin, sat down and neatly typed his entry. It read:

Dear Sirs: The word "Tiger" is sung 42 times in the record entitled "GeeTO Tiger." Below is my entry as to why I would like to win the original "GeeTO Tiger": Prowling around in a custom Tiger like the "GeeTO." I'd be as sure as a Hurst shift to make a hit with all the "cats."

Lampone's entry, amazingly enough, made it from West Allis, Wisconsin, to Hurst headquarters in Pennsylvania before the deadline four days later. He had counted the correct number of times the word "tiger" was sung, and the judges—including George Hurst, Dick Day (*Car Craft* magazine), and Wally Parks (of the National Hot Rod Association)—liked his reason for wanting the car the

most of all. How could they not? It incorporated a great sentence using the tiger theme Pontiac was hoping would stick, and how better to win George Hurst over than using "as sure as a Hurst shift"? Within weeks, young Alex Lampone was the personal guest of George Hurst at the NHRA National Drags in Indianapolis. The keys to the GeeTO Tiger were formally presented by George Hurst at dinner, along with Jack "Doc" Watson and Miss Hurst Golden Shifter Pat Flannery. *Hot Rod* magazine was on hand to document the occasion. The next day, Alex was introduced by George Hurst to the national's crowd at the races.

Alex treasured the car and drove it sparingly for a few years. One day, Alex was doing a high-speed banzai run on Interstate 94 in Milwaukee when he passed Pete Yeko, another young man who had entered the contest but didn't win. Pete Yeko was riding with his buddy Dennis Urbaniak, who had also entered the contest. As Alex blew by the other car, Pete and Dennis looked at each other and said, "There goes the GeeTO!" They tried to chase Alex down but soon lost him on surface streets. Rumor has it that Alex never let any carbon accumulate in the combustion chambers, and had mastered textbook examples of power shifting that gold Hurst shifter. Shortly after this chance encounter, Alex advertised the GeeTO for sale in the *Milwaukee Journal*. Pete Yeko was looking for his first car and immediately knew that this was the contest car. For $1,500, it was his.

Pete used the car as a fair-weather driver and even drag raced the car at Great Lakes Dragaway in Union Grove, Wisconsin, in the stock classes, winning nearly every time, as he recalls. The GeeTO was shown in *Car Craft* magazine after running a 13.17 at 100 miles per hour at Union Grove. Pete

Pontiac had a reputation for building comfortable cars, and the GeeTO carried on that reputation. The flat seat cushions did little to keep the occupants from sliding around, but that wasn't a huge problem since the narrow bias-ply tires didn't generate much in the way of lateral forces.

THE 1965 HURST GeeTO TIGER ■ 47

It was no surprise that the Hurst GeeTO Tiger was equipped with a Hurst shifter. As part of this car's "Tigerization," this one was gold plated by Hurst.

Loaded with options, the Hurst GeeTO Tiger used a black vinyl top to contrast the vivid paint.

strived to keep the car in perfect condition, and his nickname was "Mr. Clean." Nobody sat in the GeeTo Tiger unless there was a towel on the seat.

In June 1971, Pete sold the car to William Backhaus from Glendale, Wisconsin, for $1,200. Backhaus later sold the car to Gary Budzinski of Milwaukee, who was a mechanic at the local Pontiac dealership. In October 1976, Budzinski decided to sell the GeeTO because his son was turning 16 and he wanted to prevent any "trouble" from a young driver at the helm of a powerful car. Advertised again in the *Milwaukee Journal*, Budzinski described the car as a special Hurst GTO, asking for "best offer over $2,000." On October 16, GTO collector Jim Urban of Algoma, Wisconsin, purchased the car for $1,900, cash. Think about it: in 10 years this car sold for just about the same price four times. Try that with a new Corvette. Urban rebuilt the engine, detailed the car, and advertised it for sale in March 1977. Jerry Treleven of Appleton, Wisconsin, saw the car advertised and, at the urging of his friends, paid the asking price of $4,200 on March 9, 1977—pretty steep for a 1965 GTO at the time! Knowing that Urban told him the car was "very special," Treleven drove the car only occasionally. It was not until a chance encounter with Jim Wangers that Treleven knew exactly what he had. Treleven had the car repainted (its first ever) in 1982.

Now fast-forward to over a decade later to Milwaukee, where yours truly was hunting GTOs like I had a snake bite and only rare GTOs had the antivenom I needed. The GeeTO Tiger was a local legend and, by this point, missing and presumed dead. Nobody in Milwaukee had seen the car since 1976. Then, in August 1994, in the *Milwaukee Journal* auto section, front page, was the GeeTO Tiger,

Large dials and easy-to-read numbers on the optional rally gauges allowed the driver to see just how far over the speed limit he was going.

THE 1965 HURST GeeTO TIGER ■ 49

Opposite page: Tasteful and discreet, even in gold metallic. The hood scoop might not have fed air directly into the air cleaners, but it looked great.

Top, inset: Even though the Hurst GeeTO Tiger was given away to a contest winner, it was meticulously maintained, something of a rarity in the world of muscle cars, most of which ended up as piles of beaten-to-death ferrous oxide.

Bottom, inset: Even when painted to dazzle, the Hurst GeeTO exuded a street-fighter attitude.

Stacked headlights made identifying a GTO a snap, since the other General Motors A-body cars used horizontal configurations for their headlights.

not for sale, but announced as being the feature car at a local GTO show. To say I was excited about seeing the car at the show would be an understatement. Displayed on a special "tiger skin" rug, with the original tiger tail out of the hood, was the GeeTO Tiger. I took a good look and a bunch of pictures.

After Treleven told me the car would "never be for sale," I really didn't give it much more thought. That was, until 2004, when Jim Mattison of Pontiac Historic Services asked me over dinner one evening in Detroit if I had ever thought about chasing down the GeeTO Tiger for my collection. A few drinks later, we had hatched a plan: if I could buy the GeeTO, I might as well try to buy the other Hurst GTO giveaway car, the 1965 Hurst Motor Trend Riverside "500" Pace Car (profiled elsewhere in this book). In the months that followed, I was able to purchase the Riverside car and, with the help of Google, tracked down Jerry Treleven and made the call. It turns out that Jerry would sell the GeeTO Tiger, and I could have the pair of Hurst GTOs. After some trying negotiations and a few months' time, I was successful in reuniting the pair of rare GTOs.

With the exception of the 1982 repaint and an engine rebuild, the GeeTO Tiger is completely original and unrestored. It currently has 59,000 miles. Jim Mattison of Pontiac Historic Services considers the GeeTO Tiger to be perhaps the most significant GTO of all time. Not many GTOs have such a unique history, it being a real Royal Bobcat car, hand-assembled by Pontiac Engineering and Hurst Performance Products, and sung about on a record with a distribution of over 450,000, as well as having hundreds of thousands of (1965) dollars spent on promotion, plus being the centerpiece of the 1965 NHRA National Event with George Hurst and Wally Parks as its chaperones!

Now the story gets even a little stranger. Since I have owned the car I have been amazed at how it exemplifies the "six degrees of separation" theory. One day, just by chance, a friend of mine stopped into my garage, walked through the door and, upon seeing the GeeTO, said, "Hey, what are you doing with Alex's car?" It turns out he was Alex Lampone's best friend in high school and was there the first day Alex brought the car home. They used to street race his 1964 GTO against the

Optional chrome exhaust "splitters" kept the rear body panels free from exhaust soot. Careful thought was given to details that maintained functionality with a heavy dose of style.

GeeTO, and even double-dated in the car. Then, another friend stopped in, saw the car, and said "You know, that was my buddy's car back in the '60s." Well, this fellow was Pete Yeko's best friend. Later, he arranged to have Pete Yeko and Dennis Urbaniak stop by to share stories of the GeeTO. And when researching the history, Jim Urban told me that Gary Budzinski not only was a mechanic at the Pontiac dealership that my father's business represented for many years, but he also lived exactly three blocks from my garage, where the GeeTO now lives.

At the 2005 GTO Association of America (GTOAA) National Convention, the GeeTO Tiger and Hurst Motor Trend Riverside "500" Pace Car were on display in the host hotel, where Jim Wangers gave a speech on the history of the GTO. During his speech, and in a later interview conducted along with GTO historian and noted authority Paul Zazarine, Wangers stated that the GeeTO Tiger and Riverside Pace Car were two of the most significant GTOs of all time.

Now for the important question: Why is this car in a book called *Million-Dollar Muscle Cars*? And, isn't it a little weird that the author is profiling his own car? Rest assured, the inclusion of this car is only to illustrate a point. Everywhere you look there are million-dollar Mopars, Chevys, or Shelbys. Is there such a thing as a million-dollar GTO? And, why are Pontiacs in general not valued as highly as other muscle cars? I have often wondered the same thing. If Hemi E bodies are worth two-comma money, then shouldn't rare Pontiac muscle be as well? I think so.

Super Duty cars, rare promotional cars, Ram Air convertibles, and the like are all very important cars. And there is no denying the fact that the GTO brought muscle to the masses, and did it first. So if there is such a thing as a million-dollar Pontiac, it should possess similar qualities to the GeeTO Tiger. This is a one of one, hand-built promotional car that, in less than 12 months into the production run of the legendary GTO, was in the hands (and ears) of hundreds of thousands of people. The GeeTO undoubtedly helped make the GTO the runaway success it was. All these are the hallmarks of true value in collectible cars—rarity, provenance, originality, and desirability—be it a special 65 GTO or any other car. ■

Only George Hurst would gold plate a set of his wheels to use on a street-bound GTO, even if it was a contest vehicle. They matched his private plane.

Muscle cars drivers never forget that they are at the controls of a machine, not a rolling isolation chamber. Noise, vibration, and harshness are all part of the muscle car experience. It is wonderful.

The GeeTO Tiger back in the day, running through the quarter mile at Great Lakes Dragaway in Union Grove, Wisconsin, where it turned in a best time of 13.12 seconds at 107.5 miles per hour. To achieve this time, the car ran on six-inch M&H drag slicks with open headers. *Pete Yeko Collection*

"Borrowed" from Ferrari, GTO stood for Grand Turismo Omologato and was a hit with Americans of all ages, most of whom had never heard of the Italian version. Point, Pontiac.

CHAPTER FOUR

1967 SHELBY GT500 SUPER SNAKE

The 1967 Shelby GT500 is many people's favorite Shelby Mustang. In 1965 and 1966, Shelby GT350s looked pretty much like the standard Mustang Fastback, which they were based on. Sure, they had optional stripes and a hood scoop, and the 1966 had side scoops and Plexiglas quarter windows, but still, the cars were basically Mustangs. Shelby took the introduction of the new Mustang in 1967 as an opportunity to make his version that much better. He gave the new 1967 Shelby Mustang attitude. With unique front body panels, taillights, a ducktail spoiler, and more scoops than a box of Raisin Bran (a huge hood scoop and, count 'em, four scoops on the rear quarter panels!), the new Shelby had the look. On the inside, a factory-installed roll bar with retractable shoulder harnesses and underdash Stewart Warner gauges looked the part as well.

But the big news was under the hood. For the first time, Shelby had a big-block motivated Mustang: the GT500. While the GT350 soldiered on with a 289, the new Mustang had sufficient room to stuff a 428-ci Police Interceptor engine between its shock towers, and the GT500 was the result. Better still, Ol' Shel dressed that big 428 up nice with two huge Holley 600-cfm four barrels on an aluminum medium riser intake, an open cast-aluminum air cleaner, and beautiful cast-aluminum valve covers that read "Cobra Le Mans." If you are looking for a killer muscle car engine compartment, few cars

Previous page, main: Only one Shelby street car ever carried three stripes: the brutal Super Snake. The 427-cubic-inch side-oiler engine cranked out the muscle to back up the car's visual attitude.

Previous page, inset: Shelby Mustangs never used aerodynamic aids for looks alone. All of the scoops, slots, vents, and spoilers were functional and race inspired.

Top: The paper element air cleaner peeks though the hood scoop. Used as a high-speed tire test vehicle, the Super Snake sat on a used car lot for a year; nobody was willing to pony up $7,500 for a tired Shelby.

Bottom: From the chrome air cleaner to the aluminum oil pan, the 427-cubic-inch side-oiler V-8 was pure race engine, developing a staggering 520-horsepower. No street tire in its day stood a chance, regardless what Goodyear ad copy might have claimed.

The large hood scoop fed cool air into the engine compartment, while the twin rows of vents bled out the massive quantities of hot air generated by the 427 side-oiler under the fiberglass hood.

Above: The Super Snake used a welded roll bar as a safety precaution. It was an ideal place to mount the shoulder harnesses for the driver and front passenger.

Left: Chrome surrounds the outboard driving lights. Only the Super Snake received such attention.

have the curb appeal of a '67 GT500. The best part is you can catch a glimpse of all the jewelry through the hood scoop when the hood is shut—just hope it doesn't rain. With horsepower conservatively advertised at 335 and gobs of torque, this was what most buyers wanted over the high-strung 289 ci of the two prior years.

The 1967 one was also the last of what many consider to be a "real" Shelby Mustang, as in 1968 Ford took over and moved Shelby Mustang production out of Shelby's Los Angeles plant and sublet the job to A. O. Smith in Michigan. So you have the first-year big block in the "last" year Shelby, along with arguably the best-looking Shelby Mustang ever built. It's easy to see why a 1967 GT500 is at the top of many Shelby lists.

Without question, the most famous 1967 GT500 of all is an engineering study car Shelby called the Super Snake. In February 1967, Carroll Shelby asked his chief engineer, Fred Goodell, to build a high performance GT500 to be used for Goodyear's high-speed testing. Goodell obviously took the words "high speed" to heart, as he stuffed a white GT500 (serial no. 544) full of the good

Above: Since its introduction in 1964, the Mustang used a long hood/short deck formula to project speed and power. When Shelby got his hands on the original Pony Car, he made sure that it did more than just *project* speed and power.

Right: The interior of the Super Snake was standard GT500. Stock Mustang seats didn't offer much in the way of lateral support, but few sporty domestic automobiles did.

stuff: a GT40 Mk II medium-riser 427 engine with a solid-lifter cam; lightweight aluminum cylinder heads; aluminum water pump; wild GT40-style "bundle of snakes" exhaust headers; a big 780-cfm single Holley four barrel; and a host of other GT40 style improvements for durability. The standard GT500 Top Loader four-speed was retained, but a special Detroit Locker 4.11:1 rear end was fitted to get the 427 into the fat part of its power curve. To set the Super Snake apart from standard GT500s visually, a unique three-band variation of Guardsman Blue Le Mans stripes were installed, with one fat stripe flanked by two skinny ones. The Super Snake was the only GT500 that ever left Shelby with this stripe treatment. Upon completion, the Super Snake was ready for high-speed duty at Goodyear.

On March 17, 1967, Shelby American's Principal Engineer Mr. Brozek sent out a memo regarding Goodyear test vehicles. The memo outlined specific procedures for testing two cars at Goodyear's San Angelo, Texas, test track from March 23 through March 27. Two vehicles were to be tested: a White GT500, Serial No. 544 (Speed Run) and a Lime Green GT500, Serial No. 463 (Cooling Test). Shelby employees were instructed in a memo to bring: "Spare lightweight 427 engine;

Top: Legend has it that Carroll Shelby decided on the "500" part of the GT500 nomenclature because it was a bigger number than anyone else used. Shelby knew how to strike a nerve among male buyers.

Bottom: Built for long stretches of straight high-speed roads, the Super Snake was not happy in the twisties due to the very large mass of iron over the front wheels.

Five (5) Shelby American Aluminum wheels (stowed in car); and a mechanics tool box (stowed in car)." The memo spelled out when the cars were to leave Shelby, when they had to be at Goodyear in Texas, who would mount the test tires, what date the cars were to be shipped back to Shelby, and details on accommodations in San Angelo. The memo also specified which Shelby personnel would be flying on the company plane and that it was "understood that Mr. Shelby has arrangements for other transportation." Employees were told to contact Pavolich of Goodyear to confirm their actions before leaving California. Obviously, Brozek left nothing to chance.

In San Angelo at the test track, Goodyear had arranged to have a promotional movie filmed of the 500-mile high-speed tire test. Goodyear also had a number of journalists on hand for the occasion to ensure media coverage. The goal was to demonstrate the durability and safety of Goodyear's tires at high speeds. Carroll Shelby did his part by warming up the Super Snake and giving some easy 150 miles per hour plus to the journalists on hand. After Shelby was done, Fred Goodell took over for the actual testing. During the 500-mile session, the Super Snake was clocked at

The top scoop vented air from the passenger compartment, while the lower scoop directed cooling air to the rear brakes, a concern when the car was traveling on the north side of 150 miles per hour.

1967 SHELBY GT500 SUPER SNAKE

Shelby liked the look of the Thunderbird taillights, and what Shelby liked, he tended to get. A pop-open fuel filler cap made rapid refueling a snap.

170 miles per hour, and set a record 142 mile-per-hour average for the entire 500 miles. Think about the rpm that 427 was wound to with a 4.11 rear axle at these speeds. For 500 miles. Obviously, the large engine oil cooler and carefully built GT40-spec engine did their job!

The film of this incredible 500-mile test was distributed to Goodyear dealers and others to prove the quality of the new high-speed performance tires. Regardless of how convincing this film may or may not be, rest assured you will never see me going 170 miles per hour on any 1967 bias-ply tires. Ever. Even with Carroll Shelby driving.

There was also a short 45-rpm record made with Shelby driving the Super Snake at the Riverside Raceway that was included with 1967 AMT GT500 model kits. The record was titled "AMT Presents Carroll Shelby and the Sound of the Cobra!" It was a paper record produced by CBS Records.

On the cover of the April 15, 1967, *Autoweek* magazine, the Super Snake was pictured at speed on the cover with the caption, "Fast Tire Test." Inside were pictures of the Super Snake being fitted with Goodyear tires and Shelby onsite wearing his Goodyear jacket, as well as one showing him being strapped into the car for a drive. The August 1967 issue of *Drag Strip* magazine also had a three-page article on the Super Snake.

Once the Super Snake was done testing tires at 9,000 rpm, it was shipped home to Shelby American in Los Angeles. As was procedure with demo cars that were no longer needed, Shelby American went looking for a buyer for this well-broken-in GT500 with the funny stripes. Goodell contacted Don McCain, former Shelby American sales representative who was also responsible for the drag cars featured in this book. McCain was then the high-performance sales manager for Mel Burns Ford in Long Beach, California, one of Shelby's best performance dealers. McCain loved the idea of this 427 GT500 that had the potential to be a real Hemi killer. His idea was to have Shelby American build a limited run of 50 427-powered GT500s like the Super Snake, to be sold exclu-

sively through Mel Burns Ford. The problem with this idea lay with the expense of the 427 engines. Even using a standard 427, these special GT500s would have cost over $7,500. In 1967, that was 427 Cobra money and over $2,500 more than a new 427-ci, 435-horsepower Corvette. There was no way McCain could sell 50 Super Snakes. Only two other 1967 GT500s were fitted with 427s from Shelby American.

The Super Snake was eventually sold to its first owners, James Hadden and James Gorman, two commercial airline pilots from Texas. The pilots later drag raced a 1969 Boss 429 with their drag team "Hadden and Gorman." Between Hadden and Gorman's ownership of the Super Snake, there is believed to have been two interim owners in Texas before Bobby Pierce of Benbrock, Texas, purchased it in 1970. Pierce owned the Super Snake for 25 years, selling it to David Loedenberg of Florida in 1995. Loedenberg sold the car to Charles Lillard of California in 2002 after advertising it on eBay, before your faithful scribe could beg, borrow, or steal the funds necessary to put it in his garage!

Still in very original and essentially unrestored condition, the Super Snake is a true piece of Shelby American history. It is an example of when building a really fast car wasn't surrounded by red tape for manufacturers, and the only limit was how much buyers wanted to spend to have the cars they wanted made. It was a time when street cars were getting faster, and the interstate system had people thinking about how good their tires were at sustained high speeds. Just think of how many Goodyear dealers showed the Super Snake movie and mentioned that their tires could go 500 miles at an average of 142 miles per hour safely. While every Shelby is special, the Super Snake certainly deserves a spot in a book titled *Million-Dollar Muscle Cars*, as that is what this car is. ∎

With a sizable blind spot, the Super Snake could be a challenge in traffic, but when you are driving a 520-horse super car, what is behind you is not important.

Shelby has never built subtle cars. This was never more evident than with the creation of the Super Snake. It wasn't an ideal car for a timid introvert.

66   ■   CHAPTER FOUR

CHAPTER FIVE

1968 Z/28 CONVERTIBLE

At General Motors in the 1960s, the ability to wade through turbulent corporate waters was as important a skill to have as one's area of accredited expertise. Unlike the corporate environment of today, in the days when giant GM could do anything it wanted, it was more about who you knew than what your title was. For Vince Piggins, the legendary product performance guru at Chevrolet Engineering, his friends and influence proved to be especially advantageous to the cause of the Z/28 Camaro.

Originally brought to market to homologate the Camaro for SCCA Trans-Am competition, the Z/28 option package miraculously made it to production despite GM's corporate ban on racing, which had been in effect since January 1963. Chevrolet was secretly developing cars and parts for competition during this period, all the while publicly distancing itself from the practice. Those in charge turned a blind eye to the shenanigans, as it was helping to sell cars, and selling cars was what GM was all about.

Nevertheless, Piggins was constantly looking for ways to increase visibility of the brand through racing success. He did a fantastic job and the results were impressive. The Z/28's track victories in Trans-Am continued to rack up, most notably with a series championship in 1968 for Chevrolet with Roger Penske's Sunoco Camaro, driven by the legendary Mark Donohue and winning 10 of the 13 races that season. In spite of this

Previous page, main: With a total build quantity of one, you won't see another first-generation Z/28 convertible outside of the one on these pages. Hand built at GM in 1968 for Chevrolet General Manager Pete Estes, it was filled with virtually every option the assembly line could throw at it. The domed fiberglass hood showed what the next year's performance Camaros would be sporting.

Previous page, inset: Working on one's tan while carving the twisties was one of the benefits of helming the 1968 Z/28 convertible. Original owner Estes loved to drive convertibles, and when you run a General Motors Division, you can drive what you want.

Beneath the sleek 1968 sheet metal was a full slate of 1969 performance suspension components, including JL-8 four-wheel disc brakes utilizing J56 dual-pin Corvette calipers and Koni shock absorbers. Pure road-race componentry.

success, Piggins could see that the competition was beginning to gain momentum. He was particularly concerned with arch-rival Ford, as its upcoming Boss 302 boasted a canted-valve version of its 302, which was already a formidable opponent. It was purported to have huge breathing capability and a turbine-like rev range.

To keep Ford at bay, Piggins had an arsenal of new speed equipment that he wanted to bring to production to qualify Chevrolet for the 1969 race season. On deck for approval were a unique crossram dual-quad intake manifold, four-wheel disc brakes, and a cowl-induction hood. By making these pieces available on the regular production Z/28s, Chevy would be legal for SCCA Trans-Am and help keep itself in the winner's circle. Piggins had a plan to get Chevrolet General Manager Elliott M. "Pete" Estes to approve the new components. Estes was a true performance enthusiast and had shepherded the Camaro to production. Still, Piggins knew Estes needed to be convinced that the heat he would likely take from the higher-ups at GM Corporate over these performance options would be worth the trouble. Then, as now, budgetary concerns were a significant factor and, of course, GM was still out of racing, at least officially. Piggins' approach to convincing his boss was simple—he would let the parts do the talking. He would order a new Z/28 for Estes, outfit it with all of the pieces he wanted to get approved, and let the car's performance provide the sales pitch. Much like Wal-Mart shoving chewing gum in front of you at the checkout to make you realize you want some, Piggins knew Estes couldn't resist a specially equipped Z/28 if it just happened to be there.

Of course, there was a fly in the ointment; because of its performance-oriented nature, the Z/28 was only available as a coupe and Estes only drove convertible company cars. Piggins, undaunted, placed an order through Chevy's Central Office Production Order (COPO) department

Because this vehicle wore a fiberglass cowl-induction hood, the engineers utilized a prop rod to hold it up. Conventional hood hinge springs would have warped the lightweight hood in short order. Beneath it was a cross-ram manifold equipped 302-cubic-inch V-8, a race motor unleashed on public roads.

to build a one-off Z/28 convertible for his boss. The car was ordered under Dealer Code 00-500 and was built at the Norwood assembly plant on July 15, 1968. It was equipped with the full Z/28 option package, close-ratio four-speed transmission, front disc brakes, and Posi Traction rear. As the drop-top Z/28 was a "brass hat car," built for a high-profile executive, it was also ordered with a variety of comfort and convenience options not normally found on a performance car. They included a rear window defroster, folding rear seat, power windows, auxiliary lighting, Comfortilt wheel, and an AM-FM stereo.

Amazingly, the timeframe from the order being placed to the car being built and trucked to the Tech Center was a scant 24 hours. In order to make the quick turnaround possible, the assembly line was stopped and the build order was skipped to the front, a feat that took an immense amount of clout to achieve. As the car was being built for Estes, a GM vice president and board member, the clout factor was more than covered. Think this could ever happen at GM today? Guess again.

The Camaro was ordered in British Racing Green with a white Custom interior and was delivered to the GM Tech Center in Warren, Michigan. Once in the hands of Chevy engineers, they installed all of the pieces that Piggins was trying to get into production. The list included the crossram intake with dual four-barrel carbs; JL8 four-wheel disc brake system; a hand-laid prototype cowl-induction hood; tuned exhaust headers; and Koni adjustable shocks, among other items. To help make the most of the 302's rev-happy nature (and the poor low-speed performance of the crossram intake), a 4.88:1 rear axle gearset was also installed.

Once the upgrades were completed, the one-off Z/28 convertible was delivered to Estes via Bill Markley Chevrolet in Detroit. By all accounts, he loved the car, and the parts were approved for

A pair of 600-cfm Holley 4-barrel carburetors on top of a cross-ram manifold ensured that the 302-cubic-inch engine was not wanting for any fuel/air mixture. Chevrolet engineers ensured that plenty of high-performance components were installed, including transistorized ignition and headers.

1968 Z/28 CONVERTIBLE   71

It's said that Pete Estes loved driving his 1968 Z/28 convertible, and who wouldn't? The manual top sported a rear window defroster, a very rare option. In the 1960s, GM ruled the world, and nothing was too good for Chevrolet's boss.

production, making them legal for SCCA Trans-Am. Estes continued to drive the car until December 1968. The prototype parts that prompted them to being built in the first place were removed for liability reasons and it was reverted back to "stock" for retail sale. A stock, one-of-one Z/28 convertible, that is. Reportedly, Estes' next company car was a ZL1 Camaro. Seeing as how Estes never drove hardtops, the rumor has circulated for years that there is a ZL1 convertible out there. However, nobody from GM has ever confirmed nor denied its existence, and no proof of such a car has ever surfaced.

The first registered owner of the Z/28 convertible was Thomas H. Standen, a Chevrolet engineer from Dearborn, Michigan. He had seen the Camaro in the GM executive garage, realized what it was, and sought to purchase it. Buying a car from the GM executive garage, however, wasn't like going to your local GM dealer and picking out your new car. Even in the 1960s, GM did have some rules and procedures to follow.

Standen's chance to buy the Z/28 came when a GM executive dinner was scheduled in late 1968. It was announced that a select number of regular employees would be invited by way of a lottery. Standen was not selected to attend, but a friend of his was. He gave a note to the friend and told him that if the opportunity presented itself, to give it to Pete Estes. Fortunately, the friend was seated at

As the personal ride of a senior General Motors executive, this 1968 Z/28 convertible was loaded with options, including controls for the multiplex stereo radio mounted on the center console.

the same table as Estes, so he passed the note. The note described Standen's desire to purchase Estes' Z/28, and it worked. Soon after the dinner, one of Estes' secretaries called Standen to make arrangements for the sale. The Camaro was taken out of fleet service and sold to him for $3,000. Standen happily drove the car until the spring of 1970, racking up 20,000 miles on trips to Louisiana and the Florida Keys. Standen then sold it to another Chevrolet employee, Vern Nye, who worked at the Lordstown assembly plant. Standen often visited the Ohio-based plant as part of his regular duties, and the pair had become friends, sharing an interest in cars.

Nye owned the Estes Z/28 convertible for the next 20 years, adding only 10,000 miles in that period. During his ownership, Nye was involved in a serious auto accident involving a different car and was laid up for an extended period. Rumor has it that Nye somewhat misjudged a freeway off-ramp and managed to get the car he was driving into flight, unfortunately landing on the roof of a nearby home. The Z/28 was thought by many to be lost at that time, though Nye maintained ownership. While the car was underground, several collectors tried to locate the car.

One of those collectors was Dana Mecum, president of Mecum Auctions. He located the one-off Z/28 convertible and purchased it from Nye in 1991, in a trade involving a new ZR-1 Corvette that Nye wanted. The Z/28 was in largely untouched original condition at the time, but not without some battle scars. While some initially questioned the authenticity of the car, paperwork existed that proved the car was the real deal, and the critics were silenced. Mecum had the car sympathetically restored and later sold it to Georgia-based collector, Milton Robson. Always the trendsetter when it comes to values, Robson paid a then record price for any muscle car of over $100,000. He later sold it to Rich Steele, who in turn sold it to Michigan-based collector Al Maynard. Maynard's purchase of the car was in the works for years, as he had contacted Mecum to buy it in 1991, at the same time Robson had. As with many collector cars that move from collection to collection, eventually the Z/28 did make it to Maynard, just a few adoptions later.

Maynard sent the Z/28 to noted restorer Scott Tiemann at Supercar Specialties in Portland, Michigan, to have it returned to its original Estes company car configuration. The Camaro had all of the unique performance items originally installed at the GM Tech Center put back on. It is now exactly as it was when Pete Estes cruised around suburban Detroit with it back in late 1968. It once again sports its crossram intake, JL8 four-wheel disc brakes, and 4.88 gears.

In 2004, Maynard turned down a $1,050,000 bid at auction for the Z/28. An interesting fact about this auction was that one of the bidders for the Z/28 was none other than Pete Estes' son, a Chevrolet dealer from Indianapolis. While not successful, to show how special this car is, Estes' son did bid into high six figures for it. Maynard held on to the car, selling it only recently in February 2007. The Estes Z/28 convertible has once again found

Top: This 1968 Z/28 convertible was a rolling showcase of 1969 options, such as an aggressive suspension, heavy-duty clutch, and 4.88:1 rear end gears. This car clearly was not meant for long distance drives, but built as a real weapon on the surface streets of Detroit.

Bottom: You won't see this call-out on the fender of any other first-generation Camaro convertible. This is the one and only.

74 ■ CHAPTER FIVE

its way back to Dana Mecum's collection, another full circle trip of sorts for this holy grail Camaro. Mecum has always viewed the Estes Z/28 as the one that got away, and after 16 years it is back in the Mecum garage.

"This car may well be the only one-off assembly line production car ever built by General Motors," Mecum said in a recent interview. "Any other one-off machine would have been a prototype built by GM Design Center or Engineering but this was a true 'one of one' production car."

Either way, this Camaro's pedigree and history are the stuff of legends—a special car built to satisfy a particular mission by larger-than-life personalities. You just can't get any better than that. The Pete Estes 1968 Z/28 convertible is not just the only first-generation Z/28 convertible, it is also perhaps the most valuable Z/28 of all. ■

When a GM car's owner is a division head, that car will be option-heavy. This example includes bumper guards, deluxe interior, and a convertible top on a model that doesn't come as a convertible. Who cares about a 401K with perks like this?

Pony cars focus more on style than on practicality, and the 1968 Camaro Z/28 maintained this focus with its diminutive trunk. The rear spoiler was functional and was put to the test in the SCCA's Trans Am racing series.

Opposite page: Taut, lithe, and compact, the 1968 Camaro Z/28 was an outstanding example of stylistic restraint. Chevrolet built 7,199 Z/28 coupes and one convertible.

CHAPTER SIX

1969 PONTIAC FIREBIRD TRANS AM CONVERTIBLES

One of the lowest production pony cars to ever roll out of Detroit was the 1969 Pontiac Trans Am. With just 697 produced, these first-year T/As are rarely seen.

First, I hope a little history will clear some misconceptions about the 1969 T/A.

In March 1969, Pontiac released a little-publicized option package for the Firebird, the Trans Am Performance and Appearance Package. Only two ads were published by Pontiac to announce its new performance car, one in *Road and Track* and another in *Motor Trend*. The Trans Am was conceived to campaign as an SCCA road race car, much like the 1965 Shelby GT350—they even wear the same war paint. To be eligible for SCCA racing, Pontiac needed to build Trans Ams and sell them to the public. A very creative idea was hatched to name this new high-performance racing Firebird. For the right to name the car after the supersuccessful Trans-Am racing series, Pontiac paid a $5 license fee to SCCA for each T/A sold. What better name for a car built to race in Trans-Am than, well, Trans Am? Pontiac continued to pay this SCCA licensing fee through the 2002 model year.

Previous page, main: Pontiac maintained its divisional look with the release of the Trans Am in 1969. The twin grille openings ensured that plenty of cooling air made it to the radiator.

Previous page; inset: At first glance, the hood stripes appear parallel, but in reality they form a V pattern on the hood. All Trans Ams in 1969 were painted Cameo White with blue trim.

Right: Ram Air III engines used a carved foam seal to direct air from the functional hood scoops to the four-barrel carburetor. Chromed valve covers were part of the $1,163.74 Trans Am package.

The 1969 Trans Am was essentially an option for the Firebird and not yet the separate model it would become. Built in relatively few numbers, it garnered far more ink than the build quantity would suggest.

The original Trans Am was a late 1969 model year introduction, first available for sale in April 1969 as a $724.60 option on top of the base Firebird. All were white with twin blue stripes across the hood, roof, and rear deck; all had a blue tail panel, functional ram air hood, and 60-inch rear air foil; and all were fitted with nonfunctional "air extraction" scoops on the front fenders. It was a fantastic-looking package, and not the screaming-chicken, adorned, bloated "Smokey and the Bandit" second-generation examples most people envision when you mention Pontiac Trans Am. More importantly, the 1969 Trans Am was engineered as a complete package, with suspension upgrades and engineering done by the legendary Herb Adams, factory engineer at the time. There is something to be said about the purity of an original design, and while later Trans Ams were fine cars, none captured the look and feel of the original 1969 version. Again, many comparisons can be drawn between the 1969 T/A and the 1965 GT350. Both started as pure designs, very focused, and became nothing like the original versions in later years. Insert "fat Elvis" or "new Coke" jokes here.

So why have the 1969 Trans Ams been historically overlooked in the market, in spite of their extremely low production of just 697 cars? Chalk it up to a serious blunder by Pontiac, which didn't make the car the turn-key racer it should have been. The original Trans Am was supposed to go to market with an SCCA-legal, high-rpm, 303-ci Pontiac V-8, but the engine suffered serious developmental problems and never saw production. In its place, Pontiac transplanted two versions of its 400-ci V-8, thereby making the Trans Am ineligible for the race series it was named after. This was corporate egg-on-the-face at its finest.

Just eight convertibles were built. An equal number of manual- and automatic transmission–equipped convertible Trans Ams were assembled in 1969.

In an effort to increase the sporty driving feel, the 1969 Trans Am had an optional flatter and beefier steering wheel. Note the 1969-only "wings down" bird—on all later Trans Ams the wing tips pointed up.

With this displacement fiasco, the "win on Sunday, sell on Monday" idea went right out the window. The Trans Am's cousin, the Camaro Z/28, with its 302-ci engine, was raced quite successfully in the Trans-Am series, bolstering its sales substantially. Pontiac, on the other hand, had numerous developmental problems with its race program that never seemed to get sorted out, as documented by the late Jerry Titus, perhaps the most successful driver to field the Pontiac Firebirds. The Z/28 cranked up sales of the Camaro like its solid lifter 302 kicked out rpm. Trans Am sales, on the other hand, gained momentum much like its slow-revving, hydraulic-lifter 400-ci engine slowly shuffles up to its 5,200-rpm redline. For comparison, in 1969 Chevrolet sold 20,302 Z/28s, while Pontiac sold 697 Trans Ams. Does winning races translate to sales? I'd say this is a telling example that the answer is "yes."

For 1969 Trans Ams, the 400-ci Ram Air III engine (code L74) was standard equipment, and the much more stout and rev-happy Ram Air IV (code L67) was an option. Only 55 coupes were produced with the Ram Air IV engine, 46 being four-speeds and nine automatics. The base Ram Air III engine was fitted to 520 coupes with manual transmissions, 114 coupes with automatics. While the Ram Air III engine was a very tractable engine well suited for daily driving, the Ram Air IV, with its huge "round port" cylinder heads, aggressive camshaft, forged high-compression pistons, and free-flowing cast exhaust headers, was more in the spirit of the original idea for the Trans Am—albeit 98 cubic inches too big.

Out of these 697 Trans Ams, however, there was a very special, very limited batch of cars built. It is reported that eight 1969 Trans Am convertibles were produced, and this is the generally accepted number. Much like the Pete Estes one-off 1968 Z/28 convertible (featured elsewhere in this

While Pontiac had to share the basic F-body platform with Chevrolet, the 1969 Firebird used unique front fenders, hood, and bumpers. Functional front extractor vents were only found on the Trans Am.

A huge rear spoiler was attached to the vehicle via twin vertical pylons bolted to the trunk lid. While its ability to create useful downforce on the street was marginal, it helped the 1969 Trans Am look the part of a street-legal race car.

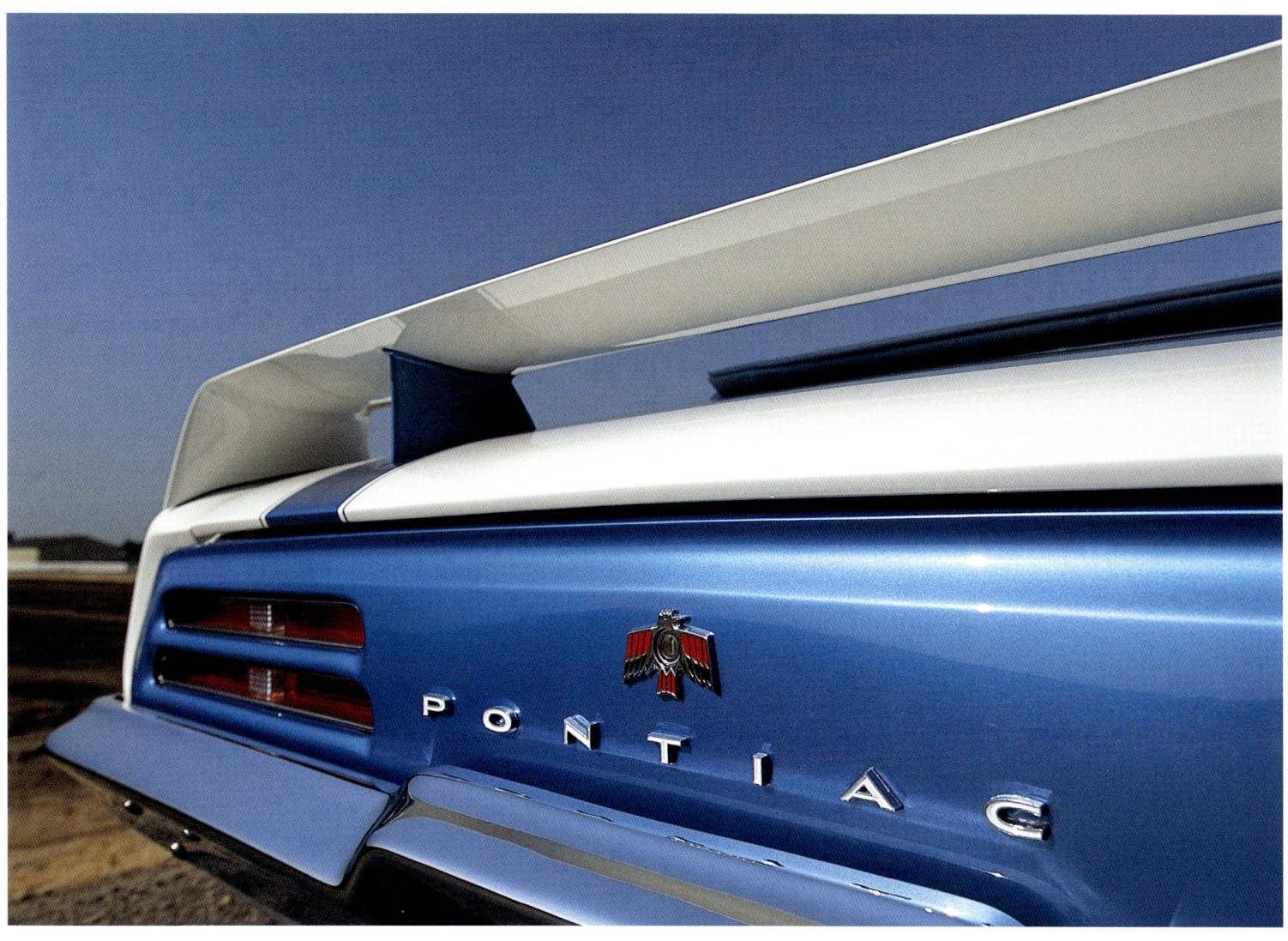

book), the 1969 T/A convertibles are way at the top of the first-generation F Body pecking order. All T/A convertibles were fitted with Ram Air III engines; no Ram Air IV T/A convertibles were built. Four cars were fitted with four-speed manual transmissions, and four had TH400 automatics. The eight cars were all optioned uniquely, as you would expect, given that these unique cars appealed to unique buyers. Jim Mattison at Pontiac Historic Services provided some interesting facts on the eight cars: none had air conditioning; one car had a tilt steering wheel, power windows, AM/FM radio, and was the only car with any of these three options; all but one car came with center floor consoles (the car without it was a four-speed); five cars had white convertible tops and three had blue tops; and three cars had the standard interior in blue, three cars had a blue Deluxe interior, one car had a Deluxe Parchment interior, and one car had a standard black interior.

For years it has been reported that only seven cars survived, but recently all eight cars on the accepted list have been accounted for by Jim Mattison. Tracking sales is difficult, as one seldom changes hands. When they do it is typically a private transaction between collectors. The only public sale of a 1969 Trans Am convertible that I know of was at the Mecum Collector Car Auction in Belvidere, Illinois, on May 26, 2001. The car, one of the four with automatic transmission, sold to a Pontiac collector from Chicago for $135,000.

Pontiac had to share many body panels with the Chevrolet Camaro, but the Excitement Division was able to create an upscale style with the Trans Am.

For a vehicle intended to be a sports car, the 1969 Trans Am could dance with purpose built muscle cars. While Pontiac shared the platform with Chevrolet, the Trans Am bore little visual similarities with the Camaro.

The scoops on the leading edge of the Trans Am hood were functional.

84 ■ CHAPTER SIX

One of the finest examples is featured here. It is one of the original four-speed cars, and the only car with the combination of the blue Deluxe interior and a blue convertible top. Miraculously, this specimen has also survived with its original drivetrain, and the car has recently been completely restored, putting the car back on the road for the first time in many years. It is owned by Charles Lillard of California.

Another well-known example is the only triple-white four-speed car (shown above) previously owned by well-known collector Milton Robson of Atlanta. Milton recently sold his car to a collector in Nevada for a sum well in excess of $1 million. These 1969 Trans Am convertibles are without question the most valuable "hair driers" of the Pontiac muscle era. They are ultra-exclusive convertible namesakes of one of the great SCCA homologation specials built by Detroit in the 1960s to gain exposure in the famous Trans-Am series. Whereas buyers couldn't get a convertible Z/28, Boss 302, or even an AMX, an extremely limited amount of buyers were able to check the right boxes and get a convertible 1969 Trans Am Firebird. Whether Pontiac fans or not, all can agree that these are the most valuable Trans Ams ever built. ■

This triple-white (white paint, white interior, white top) car recently sold for well in excess of $1 million.

CHAPTER SEVEN

1969 CAMARO ZL1

In 1968, veteran drag racer and Chevrolet dealer Fred Gibb, along with friend Vince Piggins from GM, convinced Chevrolet to build 50 special Camaros to go drag racing. What these men did not know at the time was this special Camaro would change muscle car history forever. Almost 40 years later, their creation is still unquestionably the ultimate Camaro of all time—perhaps the ultimate Chevrolet of all time. Piggins had been an engineer at Hudson where he was instrumental in the "Fabulous Hudson Hornets" sweep of NASCAR, before going to GM in the mid-1950s, just in time to help with the new small-block V-8. Piggins, obviously no stranger to performance, is referred to as the father of the Camaro. Without Piggins and Pete Estes, it is very likely the Camaro would not have become the performance car it is. This special Camaro dreamed up by Fred Gibb and Vince Piggins is the 1969 ZL1 Camaro, or Central Office Production Order (COPO) 9560.

Fred Gibb wanted a car that would dominate NHRA Super Stock drag racing. With dealers like Don Yenko mounting cast-iron 427-ci big blocks into the Camaro, Gibb set his sights on getting Chevrolet's all-aluminum 427 motor into the Camaro—somehow. This new engine, the first all-aluminum engine ever from GM, had been developed for use in Can-Am racing. Being cast in aluminum specifically to keep the weight down in Can-Am applications, it tipped the scales at right around 500 pounds.

Previous page, main: With the installation of the all-aluminum ZL1 V-8, the Camaro was transformed into a quarter-mile warrior. Only 69 ZL1s were built, and this is the only one still owned by its original buyer.

Previous page, inset: When campaigned in Super Stock-B Production, this ZL1 ran in the eleven-second range. It has never been registered for street use, having been a drag car all of its life.

Drag cars require just enough front tire to maintain directional control. Turning ability doesn't really enter the picture, nor would the car oblige if called upon to do so.

This is just about what a cast-iron small-block V-8 weighed. Gibb figured, in the Camaro, this lightweight, big-horsepower engine would be just the ticket for Super Stock racing.

The rest of the COPO 9560 package was developed around the 427-ci engine. All would have the F41 suspension, a special super heavy-duty "BE" code 4.10:1 rear axle with a heat-treated ring and pinion and unique heavy-duty Positraction unit, Transistorized Ignition adapted from the Corvette, cowl induction hood, power disc brakes, and the choice of an M-22 four-speed, an M-21 four-speed, or an M40 TH400 automatic.

While the engine was rated at 430 horsepower, it may be more accurate to say it was "factored" this horsepower; actual output with a good exhaust and tune was over 500 horsepower. To be eligible for Super Stock, a minimum of 50 cars needed to be produced, so Gibb ordered 50 cars equipped with the 9560/ZL1 package for his dealership, with strict instructions to make sure he had a car by the end of 1968. Gibb needed to make the first AHRA race in Phoenix, Arizona, in January 1969. Strings were pulled, and on December 31, 1968, two identical Dusk Blue, M40 automatic ZL1 Camaros were delivered to Gibb Chevrolet in LaHarpe, Illinois, on a cool, crisp, 20-degree-below-zero day. Neither car would start.

To add insult to injury, Gibb looked at the invoices and was immediately concerned with his obligation to GM for the two dead cars on his doorstep and the 48 on the way. The list price was over $7,200! The ZL1 option was priced by GM at $4,160.50. Gibb had previously predicted that the 9560/ZL1 package would add roughly $2,000 to the base price of a 1969 Camaro, for a sticker of about $4,900. After all, the recently introduced COPO 9561 package, with a cast-iron 427/425-horsepower

When a ZL1 used stock exhaust manifolds, power was down to the engine's rated 430 horsepower, but installing a set of headers bumped output to nearly 600 horsepower.

1969 CAMARO ZL1 ■ 89

Top: Gracing the top of the dashboard is a cable-driven tachometer, within an easy sightline for the driver. The gauge on top of the cowl shows the fuel pressure.

Bottom: Big headers were mandatory to extract serious power from the ZL1 engine. Note the turnbuckle attaching the block to the chassis in an effort to keep the big block in place under heavy throttle.

Opposite page: At the rear, drivers want to get as much tire on the ground as possible in an effort to get as much power down as possible. Tubbing the rear wheel wells was necessary for clearance.

engine, was $489.75. Unbeknownst to Gibb, however, a new GM edict put into play between the conception of the 9560 package and production stated that special option packages could not be loss leaders and had to carry their own weight. The research and development costs associated with the COPO 9560 package were factored into the option package price; hence the $4,165.50 price tag. Gibb was instantly the owner of 50 cars that car dealers typically refer to as "sale proof."

Actually, sale proof may be a little too kind, as trying to sell a $7,200 Camaro in 1969 could be considered damn near impossible. After Gibb pleaded his case and explained how being on the hook for 50 ZL1s would put him out of business, in an unprecedented move, GM let him return 37 of the 50 cars. They were sent by rail back to the Norwood, Ohio, assembly plant and re-invoiced to various GM dealers across the country. As word spread, amazingly enough, 19 other dealers ordered their own ZL1s. Slowly but surely they sold, with the last new 1969 ZL1 (the No. 18 car) leaving Gibb Chevrolet in late 1972.

I had the honor of owning car No. 18 for a short while. It is a Dusk Blue, four-speed car, one of only a few cars with its original "born with" engine and transmission. I sold it in October 2005 for $840,000, and it now resides in a private collection in Nevada.

The official GM VIN (vehicle identification number) list for all 1969 ZL1 Camaros documents the production of 69 cars. This is the generally accepted production number, although recent research has shown the very good possibility of a 70th car that is not on the list. It is rumored to exist in Canada, and GM of Canada is reported to have a production record for the car. Hopefully the owner of this car will come forward if it exists and set the record straight. Roughly 50 original ZL1 Camaros have been documented as surviving to date.

Featured here are two incredible examples of COPO 9560 ZL1 Camaros. The first car is the No. 16 ZL1, a Hugger Orange M21 four-speed, and the subject of one of my favorite muscle car stories. It is the only ZL1 Camaro still owned by its original owner. Ken Barnhart of Elgin, Illinois, purchased No. 16 brand-new from Fred Gibb in 1969. Already an accomplished drag racer by this time, when he heard about the new ZL1 Camaro he saw it as a way to finally beat Bill "Grumpy" Jenkins and dominate the SS/B class. Ken contacted Fred Gibb to purchase a ZL1. Gibb proceeded to interrogate Ken to make sure his intentions were to race the Camaro, and that he was the right kind of driver for the car. Apparently Ken said the right things to Gibb, as he soon had his ZL1. Ken wasted no time in using ZL1 No. 16 to continue his winning ways.

When a vehicle shows nine miles on the odometer, it's a good bet that the original T3 headlights haven't seen much use. Paint is original, chrome is original, owner is original. While the car can still run as fast as it did in 1969, the owner cannot.

Like any other ZL1, #16 has a cowl-induction hood. It ducts cool air in from the low-pressure area at the base of the windshield to the intake, as well as letting hot underhood air escape.

Although he missed the 1969 NHRA nationals due to what he calls a valid excuse (an emergency appendectomy—big deal, I say), he was back with a vengeance in 1970. At the 1970 national event at Indianapolis, Ken beat Jenkins to become the 1970 NHRA Super Stock Champion in this very car with an 11.61-second, 121.13-mile-per-hour run. The best part about this car is how it has been used. It was bought new to drag race, and it did so among the best cars in the country. But even after the car had become just an old race car, Ken has kept racing it, going from competitive, professional racing up through the mid-1970s to nostalgia and club racing today. In 2005, I watched Ken launch ZL1 No. 16 so hard off the line at the Supercar Reunion at Gateway International Raceway that it picked both front tires about 3 feet off the ground, and literally ripped the rod ends right out of the right rear ladder bar! And the best part? Old Ken was back at the same event in 2006, rear suspension freshened up, running his old friend just as hard as he has since the day it was new. When asked if he has ever been tempted to sell No. 16 due to its value, Ken didn't bat an eye when he said "no." If you ever have the opportunity to see Ken Barnhart and his ZL1 No. 16 Camaro in action, don't pass it up. Both the car and its owner are rare examples of the real thing.

The second car is the ZL1 No. 55, one of only two Rally Sport–equipped ZL1 Camaros ever built. It too has a fascinating history. A Le Mans Blue M22 four-speed car, it was ordered new through Whit Chevrolet in Fayetteville, Arkansas. Apparently, the person who ordered the car wanted a fully optioned, almost luxurious Rally Sport ZL1. The No. 55 car was ordered with a white Deluxe interior, white Vinyl top, front and rear spoilers, M22 Rock Crusher four-speed, center console, power steering, AM radio, optional gauges, Sport steering wheel, a remote outside mirror, and painted Endura front bumper. The sticker price was over $8,000—or almost twice the price of a brand-new Corvette! When the car arrived, the fellow that ordered it didn't like the car because it was too plain-looking, so he passed on it.

So now Whit Chevrolet had a real problem—an $8,000 ZL1 Camaro to sell in 1969. In Arkansas. Yikes. So to dress the car up a little, Whit painted white racing and accent stripes—dual stripes over the hood and deck, along with other accents on the sides of the cowl hood scoop and elsewhere on the car. They added "ZL1" callout badges on the hood as well. Whether or not this helped, Whit sold the car to its first owner, Ed Winstead, relatively soon after the beauty treatment.

While still under warranty, Winstead complained of excessive oil consumption and insisted on a completely new short block, rather than having the original one rebuilt under warranty. So the dealer and GM obliged, and No. 55's original block was removed from the car. The service manager at Whit couldn't stand to return a perfectly good ZL1 block with just a scrape in one cylinder bore back to GM, so he kept it under his workbench, later taking it home.

The No. 55 car passed through a few owners, never really getting driven but rather preserved. Even when new, this was a very special car in more than just price alone. By the late 1980s, muscle car hunter Greg Joseph located No. 55 and secured it for legendary collector Otis Chandler. At the time, it had just 6,000 original miles. Later, Chandler sold the car to Joseph and his friend Kenn Funk, who then sold it to collector Dave Christenholz in 2002 with 7,000 miles on the clock.

As fate would have it, in 2004 a friend of mine told me that he had the original block for ZL1 No, 55, which he knew Dave owned, and that I was friends with Dave. Turns out the service manager had bartered the block years ago, and it had gone from one dusty garage to the next for the last 30-odd years. What are the odds it would turn up with a guy who knew the location of the car? It took three months until Dave and the owner of the block ended up at the same show and they struck a deal to return the original block to No. 55. I later picked up the block and delivered it to Dave, so now, although not installed in the car, another ZL1 has been reunited with its original heart. Today, in truly exceptional original and unrestored condition, ZL1 No. 55 resides in Arizona and is a perfect example of the way these cars were when new. It has never been raced, cut, or abused, and is the rare exception to the life most ZL1s lived.

The business end. More than once, Barnhart has lifted the front end off the ground at the starting line. Each rock chip on the fender was earned the hard way.

Top: Per NHRA rules, a roll cage and five-point harness are required, but the rest of the interior is essentially bone stock. The roll bar section in front of the door is pinned and hinged to allow easy access to the driver's seat.

Though intended for racing duties, some ZL1s served as extremely rapid street transportation. Take #55, for example; it has never been raced, cut, or abused, and is the rare exception to the life lived by most ZL1s.

Bottom, right: In spite of featuring many of the luxury items available on the Camaro order form, the only ornamentation on #55's steel wheels was a set of homely dog-dish hubcaps. When the car arrived, the fellow who ordered it didn't like the car because it was too plain-looking, so he passed on it.

Bottom, left: ZL1 #55 is perhaps the most opulent ZL1 ever built, with a white Deluxe interior, white Vinyl top, front and rear spoilers, M22 Rock Crusher four-speed, center console, power steering, AM radio, optional gauges, Sport steering wheel, a remote outside mirror, and painted Endura front bumper.

As arguably the most valuable Camaros of all time, ZL1s are always at the head of the market. When cast-iron 427 COPO 9561 Camaros were trading for $50,000, a good ZL1 was four times that amount. Now that cast-iron COPO Camaros are $225,000, ZL1 Camaros are again four times that amount—if you can find one. When I sold No. 18 in 2005 for $840,000 at auction, it was a world-record price, well deserved by such a great car—an original drivetrain, fully documented, perfect car. If a car such as Ken Barnhart's No. 16 ZL1 with its incredible history, or Dave Christenholz's No. 55 RS ZL1 time capsule would come up for sale, you better believe they will have two commas in the resulting price. This is Camaro history, pure and simple. If you are a Camaro lover, it just doesn't get much better than the mighty ZL1.

One of only two Rally Sport–equipped ZL1 Camaros, #55 was ordered new through Whit Chevrolet in Fayetteville, Arkansas. When the original buyer backed out, Whit was stuck with an $8,000 Camaro. Whit painted white racing and accent stripes, accents on the sides of the cowl hood scoop, added "ZL1" callout badges on the hood, and sold the car to its first owner, Ed Winstead.

CHAPTER EIGHT

1971 SOX & MARTIN PRO STOCK HEMI 'CUDA

Long before drag racing advancements such as the Lenco clutchless transmission, air shifters, or even the legendary Chrysler 727 Torqueflite transmission, "Mr. Four Speed," a.k.a. Willard "Ronnie" Sox, power-shifted his famous red, white, and blue dragsters to fame. Sox won numerous world records and national event victories in the National Hot Rod Association (NHRA), the American Hot Rod Association (AHRA), and the International Hot Rod Association (IHRA) competitions. The most successful of the many cars campaigned by the legendary team of Ronnie Sox and Buddy Martin was its 1971 Pro Stock Hemi 'Cuda. The car you see on these pages is this car, the one and only 1971 car campaigned by Ronnie Sox.

The Sox & Martin team was formed in 1963, when Buddy Martin provided a new 1963 Z11 Chevrolet Impala to Ronnie Sox, who was responsible for driving the car into the winner's circle. The years leading up to the campaign of 1971 had the Sox & Martin team fielding a variety of cars, including a Mercury A/FX Comet in 1964, then in 1965 the Plymouth-backed cars, a legal Super Stocker, and an altered wheelbase A/FX car. In 1966 Sox & Martin campaigned the first and last true funny car Ronnie would drive, a wild '66 Barracuda raced as the "Baccaruda."

Previous page, main: In its element, the 1971 Sox & Martin 'Cuda was part of a Pro Stock–winning dynasty. Few race cars were as immediately recognizable as those from the S&M stable.

Previous page, inset: The tall hood scoop wasn't built for show. It covered a pair of huge carburetors as well as ingesting undisturbed air flowing over the hood of the car.

With a pair of Holleys on top of a tunnel-port intake, the 426 Hemi in the 1971 Sox & Martin Pro Stock racer made enough power to cover the quarter-mile in the nine-second range.

By 1967 Chrysler had discontinued the funny car program and the Sox & Martin team began an extremely successful Super Stock program for Plymouth. This included racing a Hemi RO23 Super Stock Belvedere and a 440-powered car in a lower Super Stock class. The Hemi car was dressed up as a GTX to promote Plymouth's top-of-the-line muscle car following the adage "Win on Sunday, sell on Monday." The GTX was obviously a more stylish (and more profitable!) car for the team to put in front of race fans. Its marketing campaign included the revolutionary Sox & Martin Performance Clinics held at Plymouth dealerships close to the racetracks where the team would be racing. These clinics helped sell a great number of high-performance Plymouths and also contributed to the growing reputation of the Sox & Martin team as the best-dressed, most professional drag racing team in the country. The clinics continued on for many years and resulted in an increased awareness of drag racing. The Sox & Martin Performance Clinics have been credited with setting the standard for how to build, tune, and race the Plymouth high-performance cars.

The introduction of the new 1968 Hemi Super Stock Barracuda started the expansion of the team to include several Sox & Martin team cars racing at the same events. Through 1968 and 1969, the team raced several 1968 Hemi Super Stock Barracudas, a Hemi Super Bird, a 440 GTX, and a Hemi Road Runner. Needless to say, this kept Ronnie very busy shifting gears. As a result, Sox called on other drivers to help with the driving duties. These cars were all successful at the track and helped increase sales of Plymouth muscle cars significantly. Chrysler Corp was definitely getting its money's worth from its sponsorship of Sox & Martin.

In the 1970 season, the team built and raced both an NHRA Pro Stock Hemi 'Cuda, as well as a GT1 car for AHRA competition. The rules for the two sanctioning bodies were so different that it required two separate cars in order to be successful in both organizations. Simply saying Sox & Martin was successful may be an understatement. In 1970 the team won 17 major championship events and was runner-up in every other major event entered that year. Ronnie and the team won both the NHRA and AHRA world points championships.

CHAPTER EIGHT

Each run down the drag strip is inevitably followed by a slow roll to the ET shack to pick up the timing slip.

The 1970 'Cudas had set the drag racing world on its ear. The competition was baffled as to how to beat this juggernaut known as the Sox & Martin team. By this time, Buddy Martin had put together a group of mechanical geniuses, a venerable "dream team" of builders. This was unheard of in the world of drag racing at the time, and the resultant competitive advantage was overwhelming. With Ronnie doing the driving, Buddy managing the business end, Jake King building unbeatable power into the Hemi motors, and Dave Christie building the body and chassis, Sox & Martin set its sights on even greater success in 1971.

The 1971 'Cuda featured here is the culmination of many years of experience combined into the most devastating Pro Stock Eliminator car ever to race to that point. In fact, based on a winning percentage of over 75 percent, this particular car is perhaps the most successful Pro Stock car ever. Specific race results will be detailed later in this chapter, but first, you should know what made this car so exceptional.

The much storied horsepower generated by the engine building prowess of Jake King has been well documented. Jake built dominating yet reliable motors. Reliability wins races; if you don't make it to the line, you can't win. The team came to expect that not only would it win every race, but also that the motors were so well prepared all it had to do was polish the car, line up, and take home the trophy. These engine-building theories and techniques were nothing new, but Jake King just made them work better than anyone else.

Few muscle cars took the long hood/short deck look to such extremes as the Mopar E-bodies, resulting in an aggressive stance even while standing still.

What really set this particular car apart from all the rest was perhaps that for the first time, out-of-the-box thinking was applied to a Pro Stock car. A young man named Dave Christie, a very

1971 SOX & MARTIN PRO STOCK HEMI 'CUDA

Production bodies looking just like what was in the parking lot were a hallmark of the Pro Stock field. Exterior modifications were held to a minimum—under the hood was a different matter.

successful drag racer on his own, was hired by Sox & Martin. Christie helped Jake King take the program to the next level. Had the competition known of this effort, the protests would have been deafening. The Chevrolet and Ford teams were counting on the Sox & Martin team to rest on it laurels after the 1970 season, and had also begun a stealth campaign to get the NHRA to level the playing field.

To say that this 1971 'Cuda was state-of-the-art would be a gross understatement. The best way to describe the car is to have the man responsible for it describe its development in his own words. In a March 2, 2007, interview, Dave Christie—who is still active in high-performance engineering for a top NASCAR Nextel Cup team—related the following:

"Jake King and I built that car from an acid dipped body in white [the stage in which a car's sheet metal has been assembled but before the components and trim have been installed], which was

begun in November of 1970 and finished the third week of January 1971. The car was built to stretch the rules as much as we could. By moving the front wheels forward, the rear axle forward, the engine back for weight distribution, we could take advantage of the maximum 52 percent of vehicle weight on the rear wheels. We just cut the front frame rails loose and moved them forward, then moved the K frame forward some more. Then we cut the rear frame rails loose, and moved them until the total wheelbase was close to spec." These modifications created an altered wheelbase car that technically wasn't one. Since the measurement from hub to hub was the same as stock specifications, the tech inspectors never said a word.

"The rear wheelwells were made from 1971 Road Runner wheel house panels as they were the largest that Chrysler could send us. Buddy wanted to be able to get 16-inch dragster slicks on the car. In those days the cars had to appear stock with interior trim and upholstery, as well as a stock appearing dash and factory safety glass. Chrysler had sent a number of 'body in white' cars to Aerochem in L.A. This was a company that did chemical milling for the aerospace industry. This process, more commonly known as acid dipping, resulted in a dramatic lowering of the weight of the body. This, along with fiberglass fenders and hood, as well as replacing any part possible with a lighter part made out of aluminum, magnesium, or titanium, got the car's weight down to the absolute minimum possible. Of course, the thinner body was very tender so we shot the inside of the headliner and rear quarter panels with insulation foam, similar to Great Stuff. This was done with a mobile unit made for doing houses and attics that Holman and Moody in Charlotte had for doing cars in their race shop.

In its heyday, the Pro Stock category was one of the most popular, as the vehicles started life as production cars. Doors opened, the interiors were mostly stock, and they went like stink.

This is where the proof of a run could be put into the palm of your hand. The person in the booth had to wear hearing protection, as most cars had open exhaust systems.

Inset: Twin magnetos fired the very high compression mixture. Spark plugs tended to lead short, violent lives.

"We put the car in a truck and sent it to California as soon as it was out of the paint shop and lettered. There are some photos from Irwindale Raceway, at a Chrysler test session where it was first run. We could not test it at home because the weather was so bad and we ran out of time. The car has no decals in those photos, and Ronnie made only a few runs. He said to load it up and get out of there before everyone started to look at it too close. Ronnie and Buddy put the sponsor decals on the car that night.

"Ronnie said at the time that it was the most solid, sturdy car he had ever driven, which I'm sure was a function of the full roll cage and foamed body panels which we continued to do for the next three years. Ronnie had his most successful year in '71 for win/loss percentage. I'm sure that the car's success had a big impact on the rule change that followed the next season." Ronnie has been quoted that "every time we would win a race, they [NHRA] would add 100 pounds to our car." It got to the point where the handicap was just too much and the going became much tougher for the team.

"People should not lose sight of the fact that Jake King did the engines in all of Ronnie's race cars. It was a built-in advantage any time we pulled into the track." This "we" attitude was a hallmark of the Sox & Martin team members and a major reason for the team's unequaled success.

Drivers could feel each exhaust pulse in their derriere, as the headers dumped to atmosphere below the seats.

Like an arrow pointing toward the bulls-eye, the 1971 Sox & Martin Pro Stock race car was a purpose built machine, not adept at stopping or turning, but staggeringly fast as a straight line.

1971 SOX & MARTIN PRO STOCK HEMI 'CUDA   ■   103

To ensure that each cylinder received spark under load, each magneto fired two spark plugs per cylinder. Things went bang on cue, usually.

The following is a list of major event wins achieved by the '71 Sox & Martin Pro Stock 'Cuda:

1971 NHRA Winternationals, Pomona, CA	Pro Stock Eliminator
1971 NHRA Gatornationals, Gainesville, FL	Pro Stock Eliminator
1971 NHRA Springnationals, Dallas, TX	Pro Stock Eliminator
1971 NHRA Grandnationals, Montreal, Canada	Pro Stock Eliminator
1971 NHRA Nationals, Indianapolis, IN	Pro Stock Eliminator
1971 NHRA Supernationals, Ontario, CA	Pro Stock Eliminator
1971 IHRA Pro-Am, Rockingham, NC	Super Stock Eliminator
1971 IHRA Springnationals, Bristol, TN	Super Stock Eliminator
1971 IHRA Southern Championships, Rockingham, NC	Super Stock Eliminator
1971 IHRA All American Natls., Bristol, TN	Super Stock Eliminator
1971 National Super Stock Championships, Atco, NJ	Pro Stock Eliminator
1971 Grand American Championships, Boston, MA	Pro Stock Eliminator
1972 IHRA Open Championships Rockingham, NC	Pro Stock Eliminator

The more recent past of this important piece of drag racing history is interesting in its own right. Noted Mopar drag car aficionado Dean Klein has tracked and found several significant Sox & Martin and Dick Landy race cars. Through his extensive research, Dean discovered what he thought might be an important car that was still being raced, in North Carolina. The more he dug, the more convincing the story became. In the fall of 2003, Dean asked his good friend Dave Christie if he would go to inspect this car to see if it was, in fact, a real Sox & Martin car. The owner at the time knew the history of his car and was still having fun racing it. Once Dave got the chance to inspect the car in detail, he made a call to Dean that went: "You better go get that car before someone else finds out what it is!" Dean had recently finished restorations on the 1973 Sox & Martin and Dick Landy

The calm before the storm. The change from stationary object to ear-shattering missile was always startling, but welcome.

Pro Stock cars and was, in his words, "burned out." The difficulty and expense of finding correct vintage speed parts and doing proper vintage drag car restorations can be daunting. In a conversation with his friend and fellow vintage drag car enthusiast, Mike Guarise, they reached an agreement where they would acquire the car and the two of them would share the responsibilities of restoring it. Both Dean and Mike are very passionate about finding these historical cars and bringing them back to life for all to enjoy. This car is a prime example of their passion and dedication.

The car was picked up and taken to Erik Lindberg, who has done concours-level restorations on a number of significant vintage race cars. At Erik's Liberty Performance, the black paint on the car was removed layer by layer, revealing the telltale red, white, and blue Sox & Martin paint. With vintage parts both on hand and located through tireless searching under the guidance of Dave Christie, Erik proceeded to restore the car to 1971 race trim. The bodywork on the thin, acid-dipped panels, assembly, and engine build was done to exact Sox & Martin specs.

After the restoration, the engine is now a correct high nickel content block, with 12.5:1 pistons and very rare aluminum 16 spark plug heads. The transmission is a correct New Process all-aluminum A833 "Hemi four-speed" shifted by a Hurst Competition Plus shifter, just like Ronnie used. The intake is a vintage 1971 Weiand high rise topped by two 6214 Holley Dominators. The cam is a special Sox & Martin grind flat tappet cam produced by Crane for the restoration project. The ignition firing all this fuel consists of correct dual side-by-side magnetos, driven by a genuine Ramchargers dual mag drive. The rear end is a Sox & Martin–specified Dana 60 with 5.57 gears. All

One of the reasons the front end was built to ride as low as possible was because the hood of the car acted like a huge spoiler as the car sprinted toward the finish line.

Opposite: Here the 1970 Sox & Martin Super Stock 'Cuda warms it's tires.

this vintage go-fast stuff takes a lot to pull down at the end of the strip, but the original Hurst Air Heart brakes have been reinstalled to provide the best stopping power available by 1971 standards. The car is fitted with vintage Keystone Klassic rims with 1971-era Firestone Drag 500 front runners and drag slicks.

Heath Hite of Hite Auto Body applied the paint. Heath has painted many vintage drag cars for Dean, Erik, and Mike. Brian Trusdale applied the authentic gold- and silver-leaf lettering. The final details were handled as a group by Dave Christie, Dean Klein, and Mike Guarise. Christie applied the correct vintage sponsor stickers just as Ronnie Sox and Buddy Martin had done in January 1971, the night before the car's public debut. This time, the 1971 Sox & Martin Hemi 'Cuda made its debut at Fred Engelhart's Hemi Super Stock Gathering in July 2006. Thanks to the dedication of a team of true vintage drag car enthusiasts, the car many consider to be the holy grail of vintage racing is back in circulation.

As with many very significant cars, after many years in an automotive witness protection program of sorts, this car has been rescued and properly restored. Even from this elite group, the 1971 Sox & Martin Hemi 'Cuda stands out as an important piece of history. It is a great example of a car being more than a sum of its parts, an important distinction when establishing the value of any car. This car, and the history associated with it, certainly deserves its place among million-dollar muscle cars. ■

1971 SOX & MARTIN PRO STOCK HEMI 'CUDA

SECTION 2
SIX FIGURES AND RISING

CHAPTER NINE

THE 1965 HURST MOTOR TREND RIVERSIDE "500" PACE CAR PONTIAC GTO

Of the 514,793 GTOs built from 1964–1974, a few special examples stand out. These few examples were tweaked, tuned, promoted, sponsored, raced, or even given away by Pontiac. It was all part of building an image and presenting a hot new car to the youth market in the muscle era. Think about it: over a half million GTOs rolled out of Pontiac, a pretty fair number for what started as an option package that John DeLorean was hoping would sell a few thousand copies a year. The list of these significant cars that helped create the GTO legend includes: the famous (or infamous) 1964 *Car and Driver* test cars (there were two) that were part of the legendary "GTO vs. GTO" article pitting the Pontiac against the Ferrari 250 GTO; a handful of backdoor factory-sponsored drag cars such as the 1966 Royal Pontiac GeeTO Tigers, the Knafel Pontiac Tin Indians; Arnie "the Farmer" Beswick's 69 RAIV Judge; the 1965 Hurst GeeTO Tiger giveaway car; and this car, the only factory-supplied GTO pace car—the 1965 Hurst Motor Trend Riverside "500" Pace Car.

When thinking of pace cars, most people assume that during the course of 10 years of production, there must have been many GTO pace cars. It makes sense, as there were many Mustang, Camaro, and even Challenger pace cars. But for some reason, the original and perhaps most recognizable muscle car of all only paced one event at the direction of Pontiac Motor Division.

Previous page, main: Two Riverside 500 Pace Cars were built, one going to race winner Dan Gurney and the other awarded to a ticket holder at the race. This automobile is the ticket holder's prize and the only one of the two that still exists.

Previous page, inset: With only 20K miles on the clock, this GTO drives like a new car. Performance automobiles of the "classic" era had distinctive engine notes. Enthusiasts could differentiate GM from Ford from Chrysler products simply by listening to them roar by. A Tri-Power 389 Pontiac has a sound all its own, especially when played through the optional exhaust tip "splitters."

Few could rival George Hurst for promotional savvy, and the 1965 Hurst Motor Trend Riverside "500" Official Pace Car GTO was evidence of that. This particular car was used to debut Hurst's new mag wheel, and the company logo was plastered everywhere you looked.

The car profiled here had an interesting role in the GTO legend even before it hit Riverside Raceway on January 17, 1965, as the pace car for the Motor Trend Riverside 500 NASCAR race. Jim Wangers, GTO marketing guru, had used Hurst shifters as a selling point for Pontiac's hot new car. Recognizing that Hurst had a great reputation among the target audience for the GTO, Wangers made Hurst shifters standard equipment right from the factory. It was one less thing a new owner would have to change to personalize his or her GTO, and a great sales tool. In 1965, Pontiac started using "Hurst" lettered shift levers to further push the point. It was a great association, the hottest car on the market installing the undisputed best aftermarket shifter right at the factory. It spoke of quality and Pontiac got the jump on the competition. Later, other cars would come with Hurst shifters, but the GTO was first.

George Hurst, always the inventor and consummate marketing genius, invented a new custom mag wheel that was ready to market in early 1965. Hurst had a true passion for making not only great equipment, but also products that were better, stronger, and safer. For example, one of George Hurst's inventions was the "Jaws of Life," a device still in use today and responsible for saving countless lives. Hurst developed it to help extract race drivers quickly and safely from their cars after a crash. Disappointed with stamped steel wheels and the fact that they were prone to failure, Hurst wanted to invent a better mousetrap. His new wheel featured a revolutionary forged aluminum center, riveted to a super-stout steel rim. Not only was the new Hurst mag wheel strong and extremely safe, it was also beautiful with polished spokes, chrome center caps, and a polished replaceable trim ring. Wouldn't it be nice if today's high-buck wheels had an inexpensive trim ring you could easily replace after getting a little curb rash? Pontiac management and Hurst discussed the possibility of making the Hurst wheel a factory option for the GTO. However, the cost of the wheel would have made it a more expensive option than the Tri-Power engine, and the wheels were just too heavy. Pontiac feared the unsprung weight of the wheels would have wreaked havoc on the ride and handling of the GTO.

Hurst needed a way to present his new wheel to the public, and what better car to use than the GTO? With a media blitz that started in late 1964, Hurst used a 1965 GTO convertible in his ads, the car seemingly floating in midair with no wheels. Standing at the rear of the car was a young man, with arms crossed and looking very protective of the car, and the building behind that read "Hurst Performance Research." The caption below stated "You'll have to wait in line. This guy heard the rumor and isn't budging until Jan. 5th." The ad continued: "That is the day the custom wheel to end all custom wheels comes rolling out." January 5 was the date of the Ambassador Hotel "wheel party," as it has come to be known, although officially it was the press party for the Riverside 500 race. Was there a better way to promote the new Hurst wheel than to tie its introduction to the Riverside 500 race and the Pontiac GTO? Yes: make the GTO the Official Pace Car and get it sponsored by Hurst Performance Products and *Motor Trend* magazine, the title sponsor of Riverside Raceway. Then, bolt a set of the new Hurst wheels on a new GTO, letter the car up, and put it in front of 65,000 race fans. Pretty good plan, I'd say. But wait, there was another marketing twist. Everybody knows you need at least two pace cars, just in case one fails to make the start or something goes wrong. So Pontiac decided to build two 1965 GTO convertible pace cars and give them both away at the race. One car would go to the race-winning driver and one car would be given to a lucky ticket holder drawn at random on race day.

Pontiac built the first pace car to be used at the Ambassador Hotel and to be the main public relations car at the race. George Hurst always ordered his cars with the right stuff, and this GTO was no exception. A factory 360-horsepower Tri-Power car with four-speed, Rally gauges, center console, power top, power antenna, Rally clock, AM radio, power steering, power brakes, and many other options—it was a dream GTO. Specially modified at Pontiac Engineering for its pace car duties, it was rushed through production and originally invoiced to Majestic Pontiac of Los Angeles on December 27, 1964. On December 31, 1964, the original warranty Protect-O-Plate was made out to *Motor Trend*. On January 4, 1965, the original application for title was filled out to George Hurst, in care of Hurst Campbell and Company. Remember, on January 5 this car had a very important date at the Ambassador Hotel in the ballroom! Talk about cutting it to the wire. Hurst took the car and fitted the very first set of Hurst mag wheels ever installed on a GTO to this car. All Hurst wheels are serialized, and these are numbered 000019, 000021, 0000021, and 000028. The car was lettered as the pace car, and in a real mouthful of a title, it was christened the "Official Pace Car—Motor Trend Riverside '500,' Equipped & Awarded by HURST." George Hurst hustled his new showpiece to the party and flanked it with a bevy of Hurst Girls, including Miss Hurst Golden Shifter Pat Flannery. In the press release photo of this car taken at the hotel, George Hurst is shown standing in the car with Robert Petersen, surrounded by Hurst Girls.

After the party, it was off to the race. Dan Gurney won the race, making it his third consecutive Riverside 500 win. Gurney also went on to win the event again in 1966 and in 1968! To say Gurney owned Riverside in the 1960s would not be an inaccurate statement. Gurney was awarded the second GTO pace car, which was reported to have been involved in an accident a short time later and thought to have been destroyed.

Unlike later performance cars, the original GTO featured a full-sized trunk capable of sneaking a few of your buddies into the Starlite Drive-In.

Beneath the graphics and performance parts lives a Pontiac Tempest. The year 1965 was the GTO's second year of production, and Pontiac spent little to create GTO-specific body parts. It didn't seem to hurt sales.

Opposite page: Hurst called its new wheel "The Dazzler" due to its zinc diachromate hue. Virtually unbreakable, the wheel utilized a forged aluminum center riveted and welded to the steel rim. George Hurst wanted the safest wheel anybody could build, and he succeeded. Ultimately, this was the wheel's undoing, as over-building the wheel made it too heavy and too expensive.

Our featured car was awarded to a young man from Hollywood, California, and invoiced by Pontiac to him on April 27, 1965, when its promotional duties were done. While the winner was likely very pleased with his new GTO, Hollywood was as fashion conscious then as it is now. This dictated that the Riverside Pace Car be enrolled in the witness protection program. The first owner had the heavily lettered sides repainted to disguise the GTO's former life. Pressed into service as a daily driver with its true identity obscured, the original owner sold the car in late 1968. The second owner, also of the Hollywood Hills, loved the car enough to only drive it on special occasions, later placing the car into storage as a low-mileage GTO keepsake. Remember, during the gas crunch years, you couldn't give away a muscle car, and if you had a great one why would you sell it for nearly nothing?

In 1994, the Pace Car was advertised in *Hemmings Motor News* by the second owner after 26 years of ownership. No mention was made of it being the Riverside Pace Car, but it was advertised as a 17,000 original mile, Tri-Power, four-speed GTO convertible. Dr. Booth Durham of New Jersey responded, as he had been looking for a clean 1965 GTO for some time. A deal was struck, and the car went to its third owner. Durham had the car sent to Beverly Hills Ferrari for an inspection and service, and then shipped it home. A mechanical freshening was performed, and Durham brought the GTO back to health over the next two years. During this time, Durham contacted Jim Mattison at Pontiac Historic Services to obtain additional documentation on the car. Mattison informed Durham that his GTO was the 1965 Riverside Pace Car and produced all three factory billing histories mentioned above. Even though the original Protect-O-Plate, George Hurst title application, warranty book, and owner's manual had never left the car, its true identity was now definitely known. This has to be one of the best GTO finds of all time! In 1998, Dr. Larry Cohen of Michigan purchased the GTO from Durham. Using it as a weekend cruiser and occasional show car, Cohen drove the car a limited amount. He entered the car in the 1998 Detroit Auto Show where it won a best-in-class award.

In early 2004, Jim Mattison told me that the Riverside Pace Car was alive and well on the outskirts of Detroit. This piqued my interest as I was into high gear trying to collect a handful of special GTOs. The 1965 GTO had always been my favorite, but trying to find one with historical significance to the GTO legend was very tough. The GeeTO Tiger (featured elsewhere in this book)

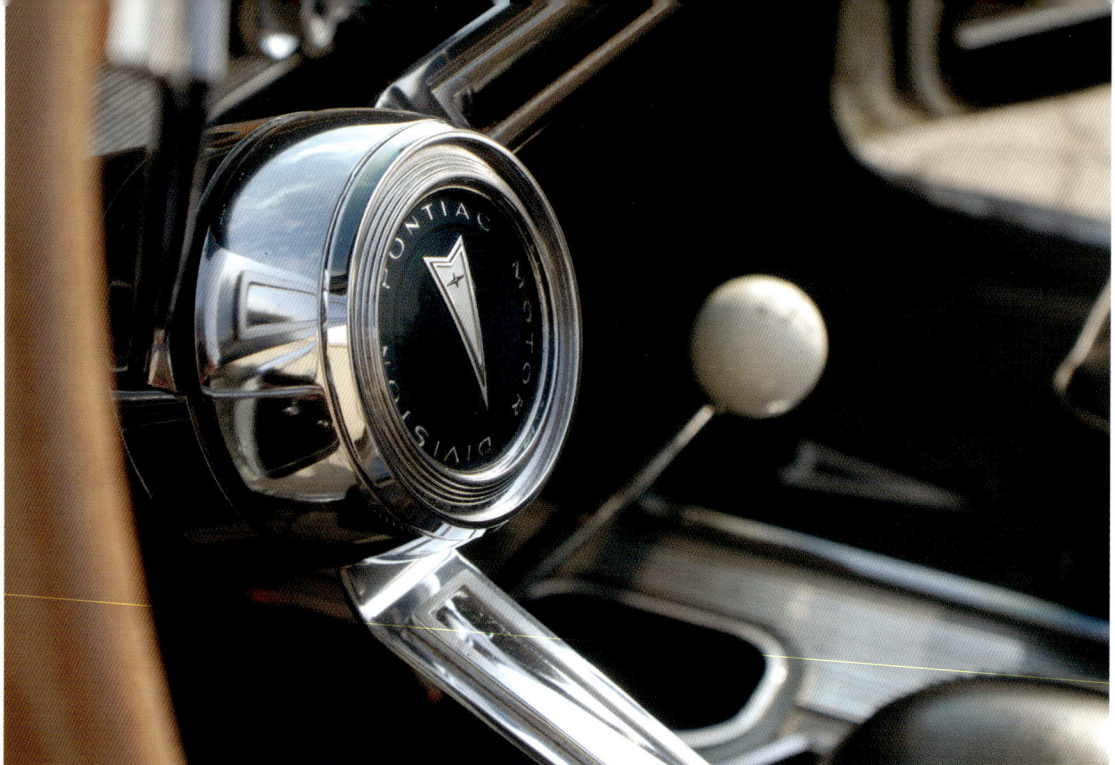

Would George Hurst want anything but a manual 4-speed transmission, in his 1965 Riverside "500" Pace Car? With tire-melting torque flowing through the transmission, a beefy Hurst shifter was a given. Pontiac was the first to install the Hurst shifter as factory equipment.

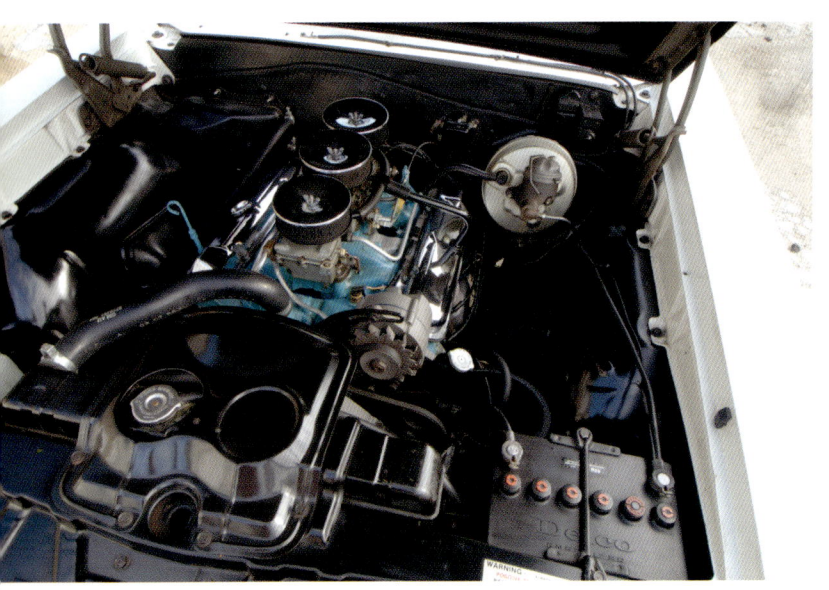

On production 1965 GTOs, the Tri-Power option cost $116 and raised the base GTO engine's horsepower from 335 horsepower to 360. Delco batteries had six individual cells that required periodic refilling with water. They also leaked acid with regularity, often corroding the battery tray, inner fender, and even the paint on the left fender when the cooling fan would push acid droplets through the hood jamb and onto the paint.

was already on my radar screen, but was deemed to be unobtainable. With the Pace Car conceivably available, I decided to make a play for it to fill the 1965 void in my little collection. Mattison supplied Cohen's name and office phone number. I followed up with a few phone calls but never got a return call. Obviously, some strange guy cold-calling a doctor's office about an old Pontiac isn't always the best angle, but hey, it was all I had!

After a few weeks, I moved on to other cars and assumed the Pace Car was not for sale. Then, in December 2004, I saw the Pace Car listed in an auction flyer; it was going up for auction in January 2005. I attended the auction, verified the car and the paperwork, and bought the car. At the time, it had 20,300 miles and was essentially an unrestored original car. The top was replaced at some point and the car was repainted. That's it. The original serialized Hurst mag wheels, the first fitted to a car, were still in place and unrestored. With the aid of vintage photographs sourced from Jim Mattison, old magazines and automotive books, and Paul Zazarine, I had the car lettered up as it would have been for the Ambassador Hotel press party and the pace car duties at Riverside. The best part was that securing this car was the catalyst I needed to encourage me to pursue the GeeTO Tiger and reunite the only two Hurst GTO giveaway cars still existing. In 2005, for the first time since 1965, the Hurst GTOs were parked side-by-side again. They say if cars could only talk, we'd get an earful. What do you think these two cars talk about late at night?

Since this book revolves around values, the big question is what is the Pace Car worth? Being the only one means it is a difficult car to establish value. But using a thought process that can be applied to any special car, we can get in the ballpark. The base value to start with is a 1965 GTO Tri-Power, four-speed convertible. At this time, a really nice, correct, and documented example is roughly $60,000. Add in an adjustment for 20,000 miles and being a great unrestored car, let's say, of 40 percent, and we get a base value of roughly $85,000. Now pop on a set of original, unrestored Hurst mag wheels that have a value of $5,000, and we are at $90,000, give or take. So how much does the Motor

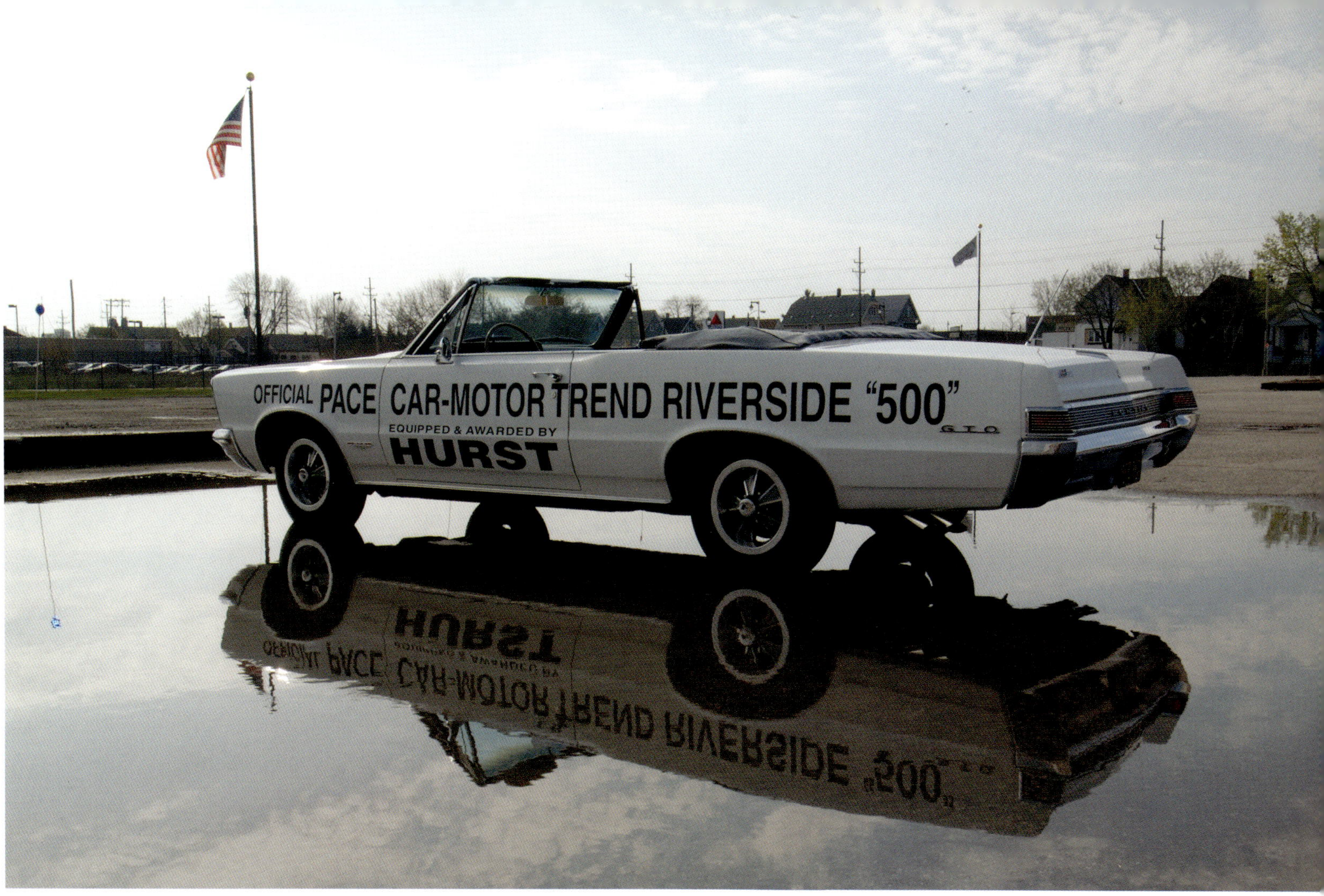
OFFICIAL PACE CAR-MOTOR TREND RIVERSIDE "500"
EQUIPPED & AWARDED BY
HURST
GTO

VERSIDE "500"
GTO

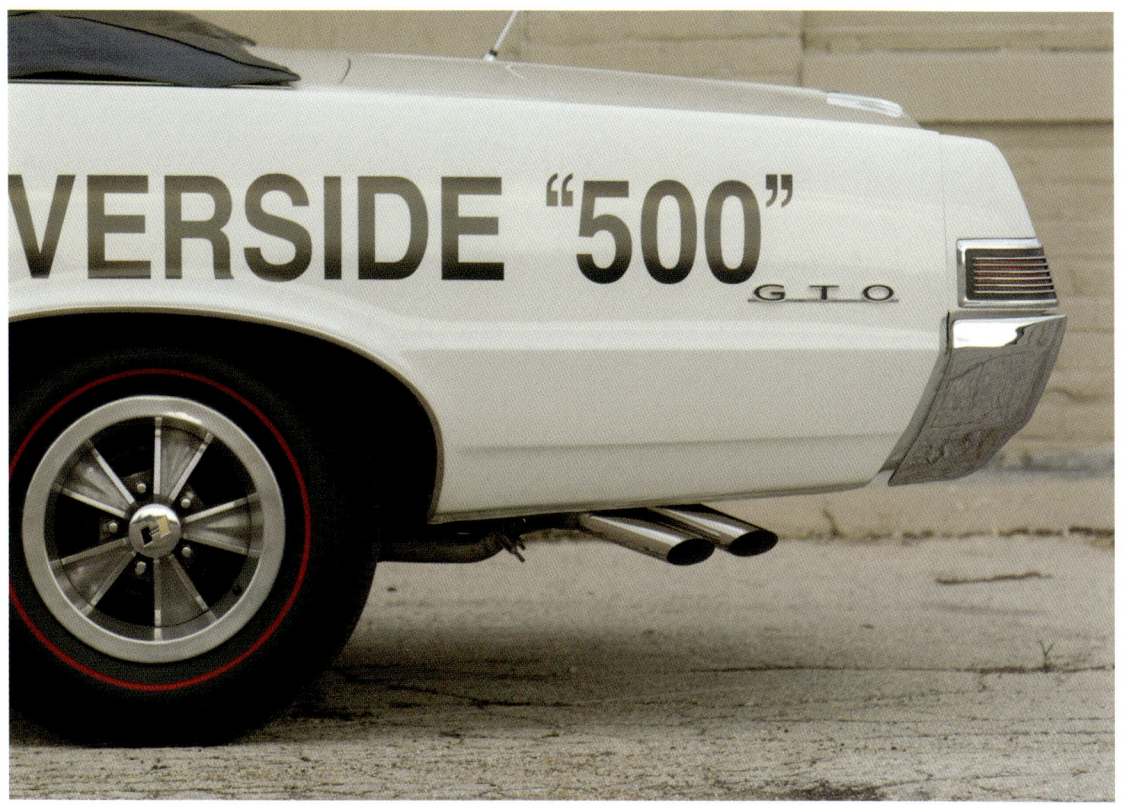

A long rear overhang allowed for excellent weight transfer characteristics under heavy acceleration. The large trunk could swallow plenty of ballast in an effort to aid traction.

Left: Dual exhaust were standard fare on a GTO. Chrome "splitters" were optional; standard exhausts were far more stealthy—simple turndown tailpipes sans any tips. Depending on the intended use, a buyer could dress a new GTO for show or for go.

Motor Trend was listed as the buyer on the Protect-O-Plate that came with the car, and the application for title was made out to "Mr. George Hurst, Hurst & Campbell Company." This was the vehicle on display at the January 5, 1965, Ambassador Hotel Wheel Press Party, where the world got their first look at the new Hurst wheel design.

Right: Unlike contemporary vehicles, the engine compartment of the 1965 GTO was filled with a V-8 powerplant and little else. Remember the days where you could actually find your engine to work on it? Note the very rare California-only closed crankcase ventilation system.

Trend/George Hurst/Riverside 500 Pace Car history add? I'd say between 5 to 10 times this amount. While some may argue with this logic, just think of what a one-of-one Hemi 'Cuda convertible with this kind of provenance would bring. Many special GM cars from Pontiac, Oldsmobile, and even Chevrolet represent value in today's market.

Remember, the most important qualities in any collectible of any kind are desirability, historical significance, provenance, and condition. Cars like the 1965 Hurst Motor Trend Riverside "500" Pace Car have these qualities in spades. Had it been a more widely publicized car nationwide, rather than primarily on the West Coast, its value would be even higher. However, due to the fact that it was used for about four months for promotional purposes and then essentially hidden away, its impact is not as great as cars like the GeeTO Tiger (see Chapter 3). With any car, the impact of the particular example in period is an important aspect of establishing value. Thankfully, through the caring hands of three owners, the Riverside GTO Pace Car survived in near time-capsule condition. It stands as an example of some of the most creative 1960s marketing ideas and the early muscle car craze all rolled into one car. ■

One of the advantages of a large trunk is the ability to stow the convertible top fully, making for a low stack height and improved visibility. Full-width brightwork accentuated the low, wide stance of the 1965 GTO, a strong Pontiac marketing tool.

CHAPTER TEN

1965–1966 SHELBY GT350 FACTORY DRAG CARS

Most people are aware of the legendary 1965 Shelby GT350 R Model race cars featured in this book. With just 36 R Models built, they are indeed the top dog of the Shelby Mustang kennel, but they are not the rarest factory competition version. That honor goes to the little-known 1965 and 1966 Shelby GT350 Drag Units. With just eight built, they are so rare that hardly anybody knows about them.

Much like the Shelby Cobra Dragonsnake drag cars that preceded them, the GT350 drag cars were the result of Shelby American employees wanting to go drag racing. Remember, in 1965 Shelby American was still just a small manufacturer and most of Carroll's talented crew were a bunch of Southern California hot-rodders. These guys grew up drag racing hot rods, not road racing sports cars or traveling to Europe and hanging out in the Formula One pits. Don McCain, a drag racer who also happened to be Shelby's sales representative, thought the GT350 would make a competitive NHRA B/Sports drag-race car. McCain presented the idea to Max Muhleman, Shelby's public relations director, who agreed that having a new GT350 drag racing was not bad publicity. McCain was to receive one GT350 with the stipulation that he had to prepare the car and race it on his own time. Two other Shelby American employees joined McCain in this drag team effort, sponsors were secured, and plans were made to turn the first GT350 into a Drag Unit.

Previous page, main: Gus Zuidema of Lebanon Valley, New York, covered the quarter-mile in 12.68 seconds in a factory GT-350 drag car. Factory equipment included a scattershield, a driveshaft safety loop, and AFX rear traction bars.

Previous page, inset: The fiberglass hood was a lift-off affair, held in place with four pins. The tall scoop was designed to pull cool ambient air into the engine compartment. If you put an address on the scoop, the U.S. Postal Service would deliver to it. It meets all postal regulations for a mailbox.

The 289-cubic-inch engine fed power through a 4.86:1 gear set. Rear drag shocks and elaborate traction bars minimized axle hop. Cure-Ride 90/10 up-lock front shocks maximized weight transfer for traction. They were stiffer than stock shocks, but not as hard as racing shocks.

NHRA rules mandated specific safety modifications that McCain and his crew needed to make to the GT350 and approved the upgrades needed to make the car competitive. McCain and his team chose Les Ritchey of Performance Associates, a well-known race car builder in Glendora, California, to develop the GT350 into what Ritchey later labeled the GT350 Performer. Numerous tweaks were employed, including yanking the motor to balance and blueprint it; installing custom exhaust headers; replacing the stock aluminum bell housing with a Cobra cast-iron scattershield; mounting 90/10 Cure-Ride drag shocks up front with 50/50 drag shocks in the rear; installing a 4.86:1 gear set; modifying the original Borg-Warner T-10 transmission with drag racing synchronizer rings for faster shifts; and installing a Hurst Competition Plus shifter. Richey's crew mounted 8.00x15x8-inch Casler Spraling rear slicks and a very impressive welded-in rear crossmember with adjustable rear suspension lift bars, then fabricated a built-in driveshaft hoop. The crew sourced a special lightweight fiberglass hood with a rural route mailbox-looking hood scoop from the Berry Plastic Glass Company. Performance Associates charged roughly $1,500 for the conversion.

The GT350 Drag Unit production consisted of four cars in 1965 and four cars in 1966. With so few cars, I can take the luxury of listing all of them and their known histories. Much of the following information is courtesy of the SAAC's 1997 World Registry:

1965 Cars

SFM5S207: Originally shipped to Downtown Motors, Inc., in Sacramento, California, on August 25, 1965, it was returned to Shelby on September 10, 1965, and sent to Performance Associates on September 17, 1965, for conversion to a Drag Unit as ordered by Webster Ford Sales. It was delivered to Webster on December 30, 1965. SFM5S207 has been restored and resides in Washington State.

SFM5S327: Shipped to Performance Associates on August 26, 1965, for conversion to Drag Unit. Shipped to Honolulu Auto Center in Honolulu, Hawaii, on October 14, 1965. Purchased new by Harry Ludwig. Featured in *Mustang Illustrated* September 2000 issue.

SFM5S351: Shipped to Performance Associates for conversion to Drag Unit on June 17, 1965. This was intended to be Don McCain's factory-sponsored drag car, but ended up being shipped to George May Ford, Lorain, Ohio, on August 10, 1965. Drag raced extensively, painted black with white stripes, it was offered for sale at Barrett-Jackson's Scottsdale auction in 1998 but not sold. It remains in Ohio.

SFM5S360: Shipped to Performance Associates on July 8, 1965, for conversion to Drag Unit. Shipped to Mel Burns Ford, Long Beach, California on August 31, 1965. This was the factory car that Don McCain raced, who debuted it at the Lions Drag Strip in Long Beach, California, on August 1, 1965. On September 5, 1965, McCain set a new B/Sports track record with a 12.93-second, 107.10-mile-per-hour run at the San Fernando Raceway in California. The whereabouts of this car are unknown and have been for many years. Time will tell if it has survived, but as of yet, no owner has stepped forward.

1966 Cars

(Note: All 1966 factory GT350 drag cars were what are known as 1965 "Carry Over" GT350 cars. The first 252 cars sold as 1966 GT350s were actually leftover 1965 cars retagged and modified to 1966 specifications. The base cars carried 1965 Ford VINs and many 1965 GT350 features. All 252 cars were white, as were the 1965 cars. Externally, they look very similar to the remainder of 1966 production cars, having been fitted with Plexiglas quarter windows, side scoops, 1966 gauge clusters, a 1966 dash-mounted tach,

Shelby built four drag cars in 1965 and four in 1966, including this example, No. 6S011. On race day, it tended to visit the fuel pumps quite often.

Next page: Stock 15-inch wheels were surrounded by Casler "cheater slicks" in 1966, and the exhaust was routed to exit in front of the rear wheels, as seen on 1965 GT350s.

and other features. Historically, the 1966 carryover cars are very desirable to Shelby buyers as they have a unique combination of 1965 and 1966 features.)

SFM6S011: This is the car featured on these pages. Originally shipped to Hi-Performance Motors, Inc., in El Segundo, California, on October 28, 1965. Shipped to John Grappone, Inc., in Concord, New Hampshire, in April 1966 as a Drag Unit. Shipped to Fuller Ford, Inc., in Cincinnati, Ohio, on May 1, 1966, without Le Mans stripes, which Fuller added. According to Ron Kaeser, former high-performance sales manager at Fuller Ford in 1966, he and the service manager of Fuller Ford were having too much fun street racing No. 11 after-hours to sell it. The general manager eventually got wise to these shenanigans after 16 months and requested they return No. 11 to Shelby as an unsold unit. Shelby shipped it back to Hi-Performance Motors in August 1967, where it was eventually sold. Originally restored in 1990, it was later purchased by Jim Ferron on November 8, 1995, still fitted with its tall Drag Unit hood scoop and other original drag car parts. Ferron freshened up the restoration and detailed the car during late 1995 and early 1996. SFM6S011 then won the Competition Class concours in July 1996 at the SAAC-21 annual convention. SFM6S011 was later sold to an owner in California, from whom yours truly purchased it in 2004. I later sold the car to noted collector Les Quam of Las Vegas. While the photographs on these pages were being taken at the drag strip in Las Vegas, Quam and his sidekick Phil DiPasquale—egged on by ace photographer David Newhardt, I presume—got a little too enthusiastic with the go-pedal and managed to hurt a few bearings in the engine. As it was not the original engine (not many drag engines survived the 1960s), through his connections with the Shelby factory in Las Vegas Quam arranged a very special deal to get No. 11 repaired. Shelby Automobiles would, if given full authority, build a new balanced, blueprinted, killer drag motor for No. 11, as well as consult the original craftsmen who had worked on the car when new to return it to exact, as-delivered 1966 Drag Unit specs. Included in this arrangement, Shelby would serialize this new motor with its original 1966 Ford VIN. At the direction of Howard Pardee, the Shelby American Automoblie Club's 1965-1966 GT350 registrar, the letters "SA" (for "Shelby American") were inserted into the VIN. SFM6S011 now has its second, numbers matching, Shelby-installed and -blessed Drag Unit motor, albeit one that produces about 150 more horsepower than the original 1966 version! Correct style rear suspension lift bars were made using original drawings and pictures from Shelby. Exact replica Drag Unit headers were made, with proper "dumps," no more exhaust for No. 11! Many other details were returned to

Belanger drag headers were designed for the harsh drag strip environment. With the exception of the tall hood scoop, there were no exterior modifications allowed.

proper 1966 specs. After spending over one year in the Shelby garage, No. 11 is now ready, with the blessing of Shelby Automobiles, to again hit the strip in the exact configuration it did when new.

SFM6S018: Factory Drag Unit converted by Performance Associates, picked up at the factory by City Motors of National City, California, on June 21, 1966.

SFM6S021: Originally shipped to Hi-Performance Motors on October 25, 1965, as a standard unsold street car, it was later converted by Performance Associates to a factory Drag Unit. Shipped to the Marshall Motor Co. of Mayfield Heights, Ohio, on June 21, 1966. Shipped to Al Grillo Ford of Lynn, Massachusetts, on August 31, 1967. At one point, No. 21 was traded along with 1965 R Model 5R096 for a 289 Cobra. SFM6S021, long since retired from drag racing, resides in Texas.

SFM6S182: Factory Drag Unit converted by Performance Associates. Ordered new by Arden "Biff" Wood of Sullivan Ford Sales in Bangor, Maine. Shipped on April 29, 1966. Shipped to Whaling City Ford, New London, Connecticut, in September 1967. Purchased by its original owner William Wadsworth of New York on August 11, 1967. Two days later, No. 182 was involved in a traffic accident on Interstate 95 in Groton, Connecticut, on September 13, 1967. SFM6S182 caught on fire as a result of this accident and was totally destroyed by fire. What was left of the car was towed to Highway Motors in Groton, who then had it buried in the Groton town landfill in 1967. As Howard Pardee of SAAC stated, No. 182's current owner is Mother Earth.

So what are 1965 and 1966 Shelby GT350 factory drag cars worth? That is a good question. With only six examples still known to exist and no recent sales, their values are hard to peg. Although over four times as many R Models were produced by Shelby in 1965, these two distinctly different cars beg comparison. The R Model cars really put Shelby Mustangs on the map. They were unbeatable in competition and became legendary cars in period and are to this day. It wouldn't be a hard argument to win if one was to say that the 1965 and 1966 GT350 cars were a lot better road racers and sports cars than they were drag cars. While Shelby tried to promote his cars in every type of motorsport, drag racing was not one where the early GT350 excelled. One has to look upon the existence of these cars as more of a concession by Shelby to his employees who loved drag racing. The exposure was great, but this was certainly not the market Shelby was after. The factory Drag Unit cars exposed a different demographic to the GT350, people who wouldn't necessarily have gone to sports car races. The Cobra Dragonsnake cars did exceptionally well drag racing and gained notoriety. This was a benefit the GT350 did not have.

Although a competent drag car, and a record-setting one at that, its success was short-lived, unlike the R Models. As such, even though considerably more rare than the R Model, values on the factory GT350 drag cars should fall somewhere in the range of two to three times a comparable street GT350 of the same year, and about half that of the more common, but far more successful, GT350 R Models of 1965. ∎

Beneath the lift-off hood was a Performance Associates–modified Shelby 289-cubic-inch engine, producing over 350 horsepower. Even though the vehicle was intended for straight-line duties alone, the full gamut of Shelby handling reinforcing components were installed, including the Export brace and Monte Carlo bar.

Shelby Mustangs are not normally thought of as cars belonging on a drag strip, yet in the mid-1960s, they were campaigned across the country with success. As most led violent lives, the fact that any survived is proof that any Shelby was always too special to discard.

128 ■ CHAPTER TEN

CHAPTER ELEVEN

1968 MR. NORM'S GSS 440 DODGE DART

In 1968, Chicago's Mr. Norm's Grand Spaulding Dodge was the area's self-proclaimed "Hi-Performance Car King." A marketing genius, Norm Kraus was a young guy selling performance cars to a young crowd. He had his own car club, in-house dyno tuning, high-performance parts department, and a loyal following. Where many dealers would push kids out the door, Mr. Norm catered to them. If you wanted a hot new Dodge to go street racing, but were a little short on cash, Norm would get you financed and magically work in all of those goodies like headers, gauges, mag wheels, and dyno tuning into the financed amount of your car. No reason your finance company had to know, right? The kids couldn't get enough. Grand Spaulding was the premier Mopar dealer, and the only dealership to offer Dodge buyers what other famous supercar dealers like Yenko, Nickey, Baldwin, and Harrell were offering the Chevy guys. Ford had Tasca, Pontiac had Royal, and there were a host of other GM tuners. But Norm's had the lock on the Mopar market.

For 1968, Norm requested a special run of 50 Dodge Darts with the 440-ci 375-horsepower Magnum engine. As Chrysler already had a 383-ci engine available in the Dart, a 440 would be a plug-and-play affair. A run of 50 cars would also make them NHRA legal for drag racing. Although this kind of corporate favor would be unheard of today, in 1968 Norm's relationship with Chrysler was strong enough to get this deal done.

Previous page, main: Chicago, Illinois–based Grand Spalding Dodge built performance cars that leaned toward the "walk softly, but carry a big stick" philosophy. Many might mistake the GSS as a mere grocery-getter.

Previous page, inset: Just your basic 375-horsepower, 440-cubic-inch V-8 and a set of fender-well racing headers. The large powerplant slid into the engine compartment with ease, though the inner wheel wells took a beating to accommodate the headers.

Mr. Norm's interior decorating was limited to a steering column-mounted Sun tach and a couple of gauges hung over the driver's right leg.

Norm was in the trenches for Chrysler, not only making the company money, but also building the street cred of its product by the day. Guys like Norm were doing what the corporate bean counters and federal regulations wouldn't let the factory do. They were taking new cars and making them work. In exchange for this, Chrysler would every once in a while bend the rules for a dealer like Norm Kraus.

Norm figured that putting the biggest engine in the smallest and lightest Dodge would make one heck of a street racing car. It is the basic principle that started the whole muscle car era, after all. So Chrysler agreed to build the cars, only for Mr. Norm's Grand Spaulding Dodge. Fifty Dart GTS 383 cars were pulled from the line and sent to Hurst-Campbell Company for the 440 conversion, just as the Hemi Super Stock Darts had been. The cars were serialized with an M code in the VIN, and all were fitted with the 440 and a 727 Torqueflite automatic transmission at Hurst. Upon completion, the Hurst/440 GTS Darts were shipped to Grand Spaulding and rebadged by Norm. So what to call these new factory-built hot rods? Well, by plucking out the "T" from the "GTS" emblems and replacing it with another "S", Norm had a "GSS," ostensibly for Grand Spaulding Sport. Another interesting detail is the original "383" emblems on the fenders were left in place. While many assume this was to make the car more of a sleeper, it was actually because there were no 440 emblems that could take their place! While this one detail was born from necessity, we can only guess as to how many street kills were fooled by the harmless 383 Dart they thought they were going to race.

The only way to get a 440 Dart in 1968 was to buy it at Grand Spaulding, and nearly all were pre-sold. Don't confuse the 1968 GSS Darts with the later 1969 M Code cars built in-house at Chrysler; the 1968 cars were hand-picked and individually converted by Hurst, making these some of the lowest-production Mopar muscle cars ever. Without question, the GSS Dart is the Yenko Nova of

Although out of favor today, in the 1960s, the best-dressed muscle cars had vinyl tops and whitewall tires.

Mr. Norm replaced the "T" in the "GTS" bade with red painted "S" to create his own "Grand Spaulding Sport" emblems. The letters may not line up perfectly, but you have to admire Mr. Norm's resourcefulness.

1968 MR. NORM'S GSS 440 DODGE DART

Even for a muscle car, the 1968 Dodge GSS was diminutive. With Hurst stuffing a 440-ci V-8 under the hood for Mr. Norm's Grand Spaulding Dodge, it became a real handful under power. The biggest problem was getting the rear tires to hook up and making sure the front stayed "aimed."

the Mopar world. It is a significant, double-digit, under-the-counter, factory-built street racer.

Of these 50 cars, just 12 are known to have survived. The car on these pages is the earliest known surviving example and is the third car in the sequence of cars converted by Hurst. It has its original motor, a ton of original paperwork, and the neat options Norm's was known for installing at the time of purchase on many cars: ridiculous Hooker Super Competition fenderwell headers with "dumps," a steering-column-mounted Sun tach, and underdash oil pressure and water temp gauges. It is your typical dealer-built hot rod.

I know the car well, as I own it. My reasons for owning it are the same as the reasons for including it in the Alternatives section of this book. When I was building my car collection, I wanted not only rare and easily documented cars, but also cars that I felt were a good value. Also, as a Hurst

Fender well headers tend to require quite a bit of room for long tubes in the search for more power. To fit such long headers under the hood of the GSS, chunks of the inner wheel wells were "opened up." Crude, yet effective.

and Mopar fanatic, a GSS 440 Dart is a good fit. I think comparing this car to other similar cars will illustrate its comparative value. The 1969 Yenko 427 Novas are trading for roughly three times what the last GSS Dart sold for. Both are dealer supercars, both built in almost identical numbers, and both are a one-year phenomenon. The Yenko had a dealer-installed 427, the GSS a factory-installed and serialized motor installed by Hurst. There is no question when looking at a GSS Dart if it is a real car (the M VIN code and definitive fender tag option codes), but it can also be determined if it is a numbers-matching car as well. To me, these are all important qualities. Would I love a Yenko Nova? Who wouldn't? But when the ink is hitting one of my checks, I look for value to some degree.

So what is a Mr. Norm's GSS 440 Dart like to live with? In a word, silly. Varying degrees of tire destruction are dialed up with the rheostat under your right foot. The car doesn't stop, and the fenderwell headers and heavy big block up front keep you from turning. The whitewall tires and goofy hubcaps would prevent Steve McQueen from looking cool. The whole deal is just, well, silly. But it is a heck of a lot of fun being silly sometimes. I've drag raced the car and, on factory F70-14

The 1968 GSS looked like economy on wheels, not a surprise when you consider the Dodge Dart was the "donor" vehicle. Light weight and a torsion bar front suspension made installing the huge 440 engine a snap.

Right: Faux hood vents broke up the large, flat expanse of metal, while lending the GSS a certain visual flair. A casual glance at the GSS would tend to lull others into thinking that it was merely a 383 equipped car. That could be a fatal mistake for its opponent in a street challenge.

bias-ply tires, it does its best to turn a 14-flat quarter-mile time at about 108 miles per hour. That is with immense tire smoke for the first 100 feet. On good tires, and with perhaps a little more skill or tuning, one can see how a car like this could have owned the streets in the 1960s—just like a Hemi 'Cuda, a Yenko Nova, or an LS6 Chevelle convertible.

So take a good look at the GSS 440. Even if you don't like the car, the basic ideas that led me to purchase it can be the same ideas that help you find a great alternative to a two-comma car. Supercar sleepers are out there, and by doing your homework, you too can find an ultra-rare—even ultra-silly—one-of-a kind muscle car for less than many people spend for a lot less car. ∎

136 ◼ CHAPTER ELEVEN

Here, a 440-ci-equipped GSS is contributing to the local tire dealers retirement fund by converting gasoline into a two-tire fire. Uncapped headers tend to attract the attention of the local law enforcement officials.

Left: In the 1960s, there were few dealerships that invested more in pursuing enthusiasts than Chicago, Illinois-based Grand Spalding Dodge. In Mopar circles, nothing beat a performance car with this coveted dealer decal.

1968 MR. NORM'S GSS 440 DODGE DART

CHAPTER TWELVE

1969 YENKO 427 NOVA

By 1969, the muscle car war was in full swing, but General Motor's corporate ban on racing and the company's reluctance to put its biggest engines in its muscle cars kept GM muscle cars from competing with the monster-motored machines produced by its rivals. Fortunately a few mavericks within the corporation did their best to circumvent corporate red tape. Take, for example, GM's corporate ban on racing, which was merely a small obstacle for those trying to get Chevrolet cars into the winner's circle. This ban just meant that all race car sponsorship activity had to be kept under the radar by using the old these-parts-just-fell-off-a-truck routine.

The mandate that took a little more maneuvering to get around was the 400-cubic-inch-displacement limit in anything other than a full-size car. This made creative thinkers in GM's fleet department, such as 22-year-old Jim Mattison, figure out a way to create Central Office Production Order (COPO) program cars such as the ZL1 Camaro. But there was another interesting side effect. A cottage industry of supercar builders stepped in to do what GM wouldn't—build little cars with big motors. Dealers including Nickey Chevrolet, Baldwin Chevrolet, Berger Chevrolet, and Dana Chevrolet were dropping 427-cubic-inch big blocks in Camaros like San Francisco hippies were dropping acid. But the king of super-car dealers has to be Yenko Chevrolet. From relatively humble begin-

1969 YENKO 427 NOVA ■ 139

Previous page, main: From its earliest days, the Nova was an economy car, designed to compete against the Ford Falcon. As such, light weight and low cost were all important. When Yenko tossed a 427-cubic-inch engine at the platform, it got people's attention.

Previous page, inset: Don Yenko used this distinctive arrow on the hood of some of his best creations.

Cast aluminum wheels adorned with Yenko-lettered centers. While disc brakes were installed in the front, they were still woefully inadequate.

beginnings, veteran SCCA road racer Don Yenko turned his family's Chevrolet dealership into a high-performance Mecca. Yenko liked what Carroll Shelby did with Ford, and he set out to do the same with Chevrolet. Some 40 years after Don Yenko rolled the first 427-cubic-inch Yenko Super Car Camaro out of his shop in Canonsburg, Pennsylvania, I think it is safe to say he succeeded.

Without question, the wildest and most valuable creation ever put to life by Don Yenko was his 1969 427 Yenko Nova. After converting roughly 164 Camaros to L72 427-cubic-inch, 425-horsepower screamers in 1967 and 1968, Yenko had an idea. If the L72 motor worked so well in a Camaro, wouldn't it be a real killer in the compact Nova? This kind of logical thought process plagues most true car guys. This is what makes us plumb nitrous into an engine that we've already bolted a supercharger onto. It makes us think if a slightly lumpy camshaft is good, then the one that has lobes like Mt. Everest and idles so rough you can literally hear each individual cylinder fire like an improvised explosive device at idle is certainly better. Like our old friend Hunter S. Thompson used to say, "It's better to be shot out of a canon than sucked through a straw."

Thankfully, nobody was able to talk Yenko out of this idea, and he went on to build what many consider to be the ultimate Yenko Super Car. Starting with a base, grocery-getter spec Nova just like your grandma used to drive, Yenko built a downright evil beast of a car.

Don Yenko knew that half the challenge in marketing a performance car was setting the vehicle apart from its competition. Using stripes, badging, and graphics, the visual component set the car apart.

The source of all the trouble was the 427-cubic-inch 425-horsepower engine as used in Chevrolet's best performance cars and COPO creations. You are looking at one of the best muscle car powerplants of all time.

As with the 1967 and 1968 Camaros, the 427 Nova left the factory as a 396-cubic-inch equipped car and was fitted with an L72 427 engine at Yenko Chevrolet. As one would expect, special Yenko stripes, badges, and details were added as well. It certainly looked the part of a supercar. Chevrolet knew that building this car at the factory was not only pushing the limits of a lightweight unibody car with a subframe, but also pushing the limits of product liability; hence Yenko Chevrolet installed the engines rather than ordering them through the COPO program.

With 4.10:1 gearing in the rear end and 425 horsepower on tap, this was a dangerous car for all but the most experienced drivers. After all, we know that even a 350-powered Nova didn't really stop or steer all that well. Now just picture that same car with twice the horsepower and another 250 pounds right where you really don't need it. A Yenko 427 Nova is a certified e-ticket

Since when does a muscle car have a vinyl roof? Don Yenko didn't care, as long as he could shoehorn a 427 engine into the engine bay.

Right: In the dictionary next to the word "Spartan" should be a photo of the interior of a Yenko Nova. From its vinyl bench seat to the rubber floor mat, it was a little lacking in creature comforts. But comfort meant weight, and in street racing, that's the enemy.

Opposite page: Boxy, flat sided, and not very stylish, the 1969 Nova was ripe for a power transfusion when Yenko started to massage it. The result was a vehicle that Yenko called "a beast, almost lethal."

1969 YENKO 427 NOVA   ■   143

The only feature that Yenko added to the interior besides his logo on the headrests was an S-W tachometer mounted to the steering column with large hose clamps.

The most lethal Nova of all wore this badge. The combination of a short wheelbase and massive power made for a rather squirrelly handling package.

ride, and is not for the faint of heart. Don Yenko later described his 427 Nova as "a beast; an almost lethal car we probably shouldn't have produced." Hindsight is 20/20. When you could get one of these things somewhat hooked up, and get the wheel hop under control, they'd run 0 to 60 in about 4.5 seconds and clear the quarter-mile in the mid-12-second range. With a good tune, headers, and open exhaust and slicks, one owner reported solid high-10-second quarter-mile times.

The generally accepted production number for the 427 Nova is roughly 30 cars, and as with all Yenkos is subject to much debate. Production numbers have been quoted from mid-20s to 37 cars in the past. While we may never know for sure, it is not debatable that there are less than 50 ever produced, making this the rarest Yenko Super Car. As one would expect, the combination of ultralow production and a ridiculously overpowered and unsafe car is what everybody wants. Back to car guy logic, you could say.

The Rallye Green 427 Yenko Nova featured here is a well-known example. While not many have traded hands, this car has called a few different garages home over the past few years, providing an insight into current prices. Sold new at Yenko affiliate dealer V. V. Cooke Chevrolet in Louisville, Kentucky, this four-speed car would have sold new for less than $4,000. By 1991, however, it had been ridden hard and put away wet, left to rot behind a body shop in Kentucky when discovered by Mitch Moore. The car was sold to a collector in North Carolina, who had it restored and later sold it to another North Carolina collector in late 2001 for less than $200,000. It then went on to a new owner in Arizona for $300,000 in 2004, and was again sold in 2006 to its current California owner for a price in the mid-$600k range. With just seven examples reported to still exist, it may be a while

144 ■ CHAPTER TWELVE

before another sale occurs. That being said, one can estimate the current value of a documented, correct 1969 Yenko Nova to be solidly in the mid- to high-six-figure range. Not bad for a car that didn't even have carpet.

If you love the Yenko mystique but aren't a big Nova fan, the good news is that you can choose from three years of Yenko Camaros, a one-year Yenko Chevelle, or even a very sensible 1970 Yenko Nova Deuce. In 1967, Yenko produced roughly 100 Camaros with transplanted 425-horsepower L72 427s. In 1968, the lowest production year, Yenko built roughly 64 L72 427 converted Camaros. And by 1969, Chevrolet was working with Yenko and supplied 201 factory L72 427-equipped COPO 9561 Camaros to Yenko that were converted into Yenko Camaros. Pick the year of Yenko Camaro you like the most, because all of them cost about the same money—right around $350,000.

In 1969, Yenko also produced approximately 99 Yenko L72-powered Chevelles, another factory COPO car from Chevrolet. A good Yenko Chevelle will be priced just shy of a good Yenko Camaro. And, in 1970, Yenko's answer to high insurance rates—the LT1 350-cubic-inch-powered Yenko Nova Deuce—hit the scene with roughly 120 produced. If you want one of these great little cars with an engine far better suited to the Nova chassis, budget around $125k to put one of these in your garage.

Whether you pick the diabolical 427 Yenko Nova or another one of Don Yenko's famous supercars, you will be driving a true muscle car icon. ■

The Yenko Nova was a simple machine with a simple purpose—go in a straight line as fast as possible. Many a Yenko Nova driver wished for clean underwear after a strong jab with the right foot, as the car tended to go where it wanted.

The Yenko Nova had the aerodynamic characteristics of the broad side of a barn, but with a 427 under the flat hood, it was a very fast barn.

Yenko started with Nova SS 396s, yanked the engine, then slid in the 427. To recoup some cost, he'd sell the "new" 396 over the counter.

With a 4.10:1 rear axle ratio, the Yenko Nova might not have been the ideal vehicle to make grocery runs, but it would allow the 427 to operate in its power band when the whip was cracked.

CHAPTER THIRTEEN

1969 DODGE CHARGER DAYTONA HEMI

The new-for-1968 Charger looked great and proved to be a sales success for Dodge. How successful? At nearly 100,000 cars, sales of the 1968 Charger were up 600 percent from the 1967 model it replaced.

Like the rest of the big three in the late 1960s, Chrysler knew it had to have its cars in front of race fans to really stimulate sales. The Charger was no exception; it needed to race. The only problem was that in spite of its good looks, the car was the aerodynamic equivalent of the proverbial brick. In NASCAR, this just didn't work. The last thing the Charger needed was to have its clock cleaned by the front-running Fords of the day.

To prevent this, Dodge decided to make a few tweaks to the Charger and smooth out the aerodynamics a little. It called in Creative Industries of Detroit to see what it could do with a Charger R/T. Creative changed the recessed Charger grille, which acted like a parachute at high speeds, into a flush mounted grille sourced from the Coronet, along with the Coronet's fixed headlamps, which replaced the Charger's standard hideaway units. Creative also opened up the recessed rear window, with its attractive sail panels, and replaced it with a leaded-steel plug and a flush mounted rear window. The result of this nip and tuck procedure was a car that was stable at high speeds, if not as attractive as the car upon which it was based. Introduced on September 1, 1968, as a 1969 model, Dodge

Previous page, main: In race trim, the Hemi-equipped Daytona could bust past 200 miles per hour. The slippery Daytona cut a startling figure on the road and the track.

Previous page, inset: The height of the rear wing was dictated by the need to open the trunk. The wind-cutting nose meant that the radiator got most of its cooling air from beneath the car, an aerodynamic design in wide use today.

For sheer outrageousness, no muscle car could surpass the 1969 Dodge Daytona Hemi. This came from an era when stock car racing actually used stock cars, and in order to put a design on the track, the manufactures had to put it on the street.

called its NASCAR special the Charger 500. Although technically 500 cars were required to be produced to homologate the model for NASCAR, in the end approximately 392 cars were built, including 67 426 Hemi-powered Charger 500s.

However good the Charger 500 was, its success on the high banks was short-lived. Ford quickly produced the 1969 Torino Talladega and 1969 Mercury Cyclone Spoiler, aerodynamically refined cars that were even better at slicing through the air than the Charger 500. The Ford cars were good enough to beat the Charger at its own game, even on the high banks of Daytona.

So the "good guys in the white hats" went back to the drawing board, or at least back to Creative Industries, to make an even more slippery Charger. This was the beginning of perhaps the wildest cars ever to be sold in Chrysler showrooms, the "Winged Warriors." Starting with the Charger 500, Creative Industries built the Charger Daytona, a car designed to break the 200-mile-per-hour barrier. To homologate the car for NASCAR, 500 copies had to be built.

The conversion from Charger 500 to Charger Daytona consisted of a lot more than a grille change and a flush rear window. Dodge was serious about aerodynamics and beating Ford. The Charger's front fenders and hood were stretched and tapered down to the front edge. A wild steel nose cone with vacuum-operated pop-up headlamps was fitted, and included a lower chin spoiler and a small mesh grille opening to feed the radiator air. Rear-facing front fender scoops above the front tires were not added for airflow, but rather for tire clearance on race versions. Creative Industries retained the rear window plug and flush mounted glass from the 500, but an incredible rear wing was added at the trailing edge of the quarter panels.

Love it or hate it, the car really did work in spite of its looks. Dodge had built a true 200-mile-per-hour weapon. On the track, the Charger Daytona was unbeatable, routinely clocking speeds

Dodge fitted driving lights inside the small nose opening on the Daytona. Flip-up headlights were installed for night driving duties. Parking the long-nosed Daytona was often done using the bump and feel method and perhaps some form of prayer.

Tests showed that the bullet-shaped nose delivered 200 pounds of downforce, while the tall tail spoiler pushed down with 600 pounds of force. On a superspeedway, that could make all the difference between winning and losing.

Dodge used very discreet badging on the 1969 Daytona, figuring that the wild design spoke volumes. The reversed scoop on top of the fender was nonfunctional on the street cars, but race cars used it for tire clearance.

approaching 200 miles per hour. On March 24, 1970, Buddy Baker broke the 200-mile-per-hour barrier, the first official lap at that speed ever in NASCAR. Later, on a frigid day at Talladega on November 24, 1970, Bobby Isaac recorded a record 201.10-mile-per-hour lap with the Charger Daytona.

In the showroom, the 503 street versions produced didn't move nearly as fast. What looked good on the high-banked ovals of NASCAR looked downright stupid in the showroom. In the car business, we say cars that don't sell have too much glue on the tires. Well, in the case of the Dodge

Only 70 of the 503 Daytonas built in 1969 were equipped with the potent Hemi engine. Displacing 426 ci, it was not exactly happy lugging around town, but get it on the highway, and the powerplant came alive.

Charger Daytona and the Plymouth Superbird that followed, these things just plain grew roots. How bad were sales? To give you an idea, in 2004 I purchased both a brand-new 1969 Daytona *and* a 1970 Superbird (the version of the car Creative Industries created for Plymouth), both from their original dealers, both being "new" unsold cars that never left the dealership. For over 34 years! Now that is what I call a floor plan.

In a strange twist of fate, the 503 1969 Charger Daytonas and 1,971 1970 Plymouth Superbirds that were once virtually sale-proof are now among the most desired muscle cars today. Once again, time heals all wounds and what was just too ridiculous to drive in the 1970s is just crazy enough to earn respect today.

Out of the 503 Charger Daytonas produced, just 70 cars had the 426 Hemi—22 with four-speed transmissions and 48 with automatics. The remaining Daytonas were 440/4 Barrel, 375-horsepower cars, the standard Daytona engine and only other available powerplant besides the Hemi. As you may have guessed, the Hemi Daytonas are the top dog of the wing car world, selling for well into the six-figure range for some time now.

Structural reinforcements were used to support the long nose of the Daytona. With the engine set so far back from the leading edge of the engine, it was essential for the radiator to get as much airflow as possible.

The T5 Copper Metallic example on these pages has a very interesting story. Ordered new by a body shop owner from Watertown Dodge in Watertown, Wisconsin, it was spec'd out with the 426 Hemi, four-speed transmission, and a bright white interior. Upon arrival to Watertown Dodge, the original buyer recalls he was disgusted with the car. Creative Industries was known for terrible workmanship, including horrendous paint matching and masking, cobbled-up wiring and hardware, and many other things acceptable to racers but not to new car buyers.

This Daytona was no exception. The car was delivered with a mismatched nose cone and a terribly dirty white interior reportedly covered in inches of dirt and dust. Refusing to keep the car, the first owner rejected it, and it was later traded to another Milwaukee area dealer, then sold to its first owner. The Daytona was apparently used quite hard, as the original motor quickly met its demise. A new motor was put in under warranty, and it too was promptly "blowed up," as the Mopar guys say. Moving on to its second owner, the Daytona acquired a standard 440/4 Magnum motor in place of the wounded Hemi.

In March 1978, Cal Anderson of Milwaukee, Wisconsin, purchased the now 440-motivated Daytona for the whopping sum of $5,000. Included was the original warranty block in need of repair.

Cal drove the Daytona for a little over two years, including a trip to the *Car Craft* Street Machine Nationals in June 1980. There, it ended up in a parking lot with the other Hemi four-speed T5 Copper Metallic Daytona, formerly of the Otis Chandler collection and now in the hands of well-known Mopar collector Tim Wellborn. After driving his Daytona to the show, Cal decided to take it home and do a "quick" restoration. The car was completely torn down, its shell was acid-dipped, and then it was left to sit because other Mopars demanded Cal's attention.

Inside, all was stock Charger. Lavish interiors were never a hallmark of the Charger line-up, and the Daytona was no exception. Dodge put the money where it would win races: in the aerodynamics and under the hood.

The years rolled on and all the usual suspects—moves, family, jobs—took precedent over restoring the old Daytona. As time went by, Cal collected parts and picked away at the car as time allowed, but nothing happened too quickly. I know, because I worked with Cal at a Chrysler-Plymouth dealership in the early 1990s, and although I often heard about this mythical Daytona, I never saw it, though I saw various parts of it getting restored.

Finally, in the fall of 2004, Cal hit the restoration hard and vowed to get the car back on the road. In 2005, after 25 years in the making, Cal had the Daytona restored, with the warranty Hemi back between the front fenders, and even made it to the Mopar Nationals. In the fall of 2005, Cal sold the Daytona he bought almost three decades earlier to a muscle car broker for well over a half million dollars. Since that sale, this particular Daytona has had more owners in a year than it had had its whole life leading up to Cal's sale. The broker "flipped" it to another broker, who sold it to a collector, who traded it to another well-known Mopar collector at a reported price of $800,000. By January 2006, the car was a resident of sunny Arizona. But not for long. By January 2007, it had been consigned to the Barrett-Jackson Scottsdale auction along with the owner's Hemi Superbird, to be sold as a pair for one price. This proved to be a poor marketing decision, as the pair of Hemi wing cars sold for just $750,000, plus the 10 percent buyer's commission, for a total of $825,000. It was a once-in-a-lifetime, buy-one-Hemi-Daytona-get-a-Hemi-Superbird-free sale.

And the buyer? He plans to split the pair up and sell them individually. Time will tell if the Barrett-Jackson sale was market correct, or if it was just a bad day to sell Hemi wing cars. Whatever the outcome, one thing is for sure: the 1969 Charger Daytonas are solid six-figure muscle and the 22 Hemi four-speed versions are indeed the king of all of the Winged Warriors, the wildest Mopar specials ever built, and the first 200-mile-per-hour cars to ever be unleashed on NASCAR's racetracks. ∎

On the salt flats at Bonneville, Utah, Bobby Isaac drove a Daytona race car to 217 miles per hour.

CHAPTER FOURTEEN

1969–1971 PONTIAC GTO JUDGE ROUND-PORT CONVERTIBLES

The rarest GM A-Body convertible muscle car is the Pontiac GTO with the Judge package. How rare? Just 293 Judge convertibles were produced during all three years of production. Compare that number to the 10,711 hardtop Judges produced during the same three model years. Fewer than 3 percent of all the Judge buyers wanted to get sunburns. This is surprising, since the convertible option only added roughly $200 to the base price of the hardtop.

The production breakdown for the three model years was as follows:

1969: 108 cars
1970: 168 cars
1971: 17 cars

Of these ultra-rare Judge drop-tops, a special group stands out as being perhaps the epitome of the ultimate Pontiac muscle car—the round-port Ram Air IV cars. In 1969 and 1970 the base Judge engine was the 400-ci, 366-horsepower Ram Air III engine, which featured a 10.75:1 compression ratio, special ram air cast exhaust manifolds, an application-specific Rochester Quadrajet carburetor, a special ram air grind camshaft, and, of course, the ram air induction system. The Ram Air III engine used the standard 400 D-port heads, named for obvious; the ports were shaped similar to an uppercase "D."

Previous page, main: It's evident that stylists rather than aerodynamists were responsible for the Judge. Pontiac's Wide Track styling was alive and well for model year 1970.

Previous page, inset: Where pony cars tended to have rear seats fit for small children and groceries, General Motors' A-body line-up could seat five real adults in style, if perhaps not in extreme comfort.

Engine call-outs flanking the functional hood scoops were the only visual indication that Pontiac's hottest engine was simmering below.

A 3.55:1 rear axle gear ratio was standard as well, and buyers had their choice of transmissions and other options. The Ram Air III was a solid performer. However, truly power-hungry Judge buyers had the option of ordering the Ram Air IV engine in place of the base Ram Air III. A pricey option at over $500, it did include some really good stuff. The Ram Air III D-port heads were replaced by free-flowing round-port heads. The cast-iron Ram Air III intake manifold with integral carburetor heat crossover was replaced with a trick aluminum Ram Air IV two-piece version with a separate heat crossover. A Ram Air IV spec cam was installed along with a special high-rpm valvetrain. A special distributor and recalibrated carburetor were used, and the entire bottom end was special, with four-bolt main bearing caps held in a special Arma-Steel crank and connecting rods swinging forged steel pistons. The oiling system was also modified, and round-port versions of the special Ram Air III exhaust manifolds were used. Along with the Ram Air IV option came a steeper 3.90:1 rear axle gear ratio as standard, with the stump pulling 4.33:1 optional. To handle the increased power, a four-pinion heavy-duty limited slip differential replaced the two-pinion one used with lower numerical gears.

In a move surely intended to help young buyers with insurance premiums, Pontiac did make a serious marketing blunder. It underrated the expensive Ram Air IV engine option at 370 horsepower, versus the 366 rating of the Ram Air III. To buyers used to grandiose claims of factory horsepower, a mere 4 additional horsepower for an extra 500 bucks didn't seen too inviting, which obviously did not help sales of the Ram Air IV option.

Partly because of this, very few of the already rare Judge convertibles left Pontiac with a Ram Air IV under their hoods. In 1969, just five Ram Air IV Judge convertibles were produced, all of them four-speeds, and only three of them are known to have survived. In 1970, although exact Ram Air IV Judge convertible production numbers are not known, we can get a rough idea by looking at the bigger picture. Thirty-seven GTO convertibles were produced with the Ram Air IV option, including Judges. While the number "14" has been quoted for Ram Air IV 1970 Judge convertibles, as of now there is no hard-and-fast number. What we do know is that currently there are seven

Bold styling was once a given from General Motors designers. Kids could identify GM cars at night a hundred yards away.

Care needed to be used to ensure that the Ram Air IV's power was used for the forces of good. With 370 horsepower, a license suspension was just a flex of the right foot away.

1969-1971 PONTIAC GTO JUDGE ROUND-PORT CONVERTIBLES

With approximately 14 1970 Judge Ram Air IV 4-speed ragtops built, the odds were low that you'd pull up next to one at a stoplight.

Body-colored Endura front bumper contributed to a sleek nose, while wheel arch graphics lent a psychedelic flavor to the Judge—perfect for the times.

documented Ram Air IV automatic and five documented Ram Air IV four-speed 1970 Judge convertibles. There are likely more, and obviously some have been destroyed in the 37 years since they left Pontiac. Whatever the exact number may be, it is certainly far less than 37 and more likely in the 15–20 range. Rare indeed.

Let's take a look at values. With so few cars produced, and an even smaller number that have survived, it is not an easy market to track. Add to this the fact that the vast majority of the remaining cars are not restored but rather are in need of a restoration, and it gets even harder to place a value on a "done" car.

Two of the three remaining 1969 Ram Air IV Judge convertibles are restored. One is a triple-black car that is truly stunning, a perfect restoration, and dressed appropriately for a Judge in all black. It is owned by noted Pontiac collector Milton Robson. This car is a real wild card; if it ever gets offered for sale it will be the first 1969 Ram Air IV Judge convertible to go to market for many years. We all know what Milton did a few years back with his 1971 Hemi 'Cuda convertible and his ad in *Hemmings Motor News* asking for a cool million bucks. While I do not think this Judge is worth that kind of money, I wouldn't be at all surprised to see it bring a record price in the $600,000–$700,000 range.

The Palladium Silver 1970 car featured on these pages gives us an even-better story. This car surfaced for sale in my neck of the woods in approximately 2001–2002 as a restorable but rough basket case. The owner at the time reportedly paid well under $50,000 for the car a few years prior. It no longer

had its original engine or various other specialized Ram Air IV components, but it was a reasonably solid car. The owner sold it in 2002 for a then record price of around $125,000, which sent ripples through the Pontiac community even though it was not publicized.

The same purchaser of this silver car purchased another Ram Air IV 1970 Judge convertible a year later for roughly the same money. In late 2004, the silver car made its way to a collector in Arizona for approximately $300,000, still unrestored. In 2005, the silver car was given a full concours restoration and is now among the finest Ram Air IV Judges in existence. The only four-speed car known in silver, it is also a nicely equipped car with a factory hood tach, Custom Sport steering wheel, power steering, power disc brakes, and a few other nice factory options. I would peg its current value in the same range as the 1969, roughly $600,000–$700,000. Although the 1970 was a higher-production car and we do not know the exact production totals, most buyers are partial to the styling of the 1970 model year. This balances out with the lower production and arguably better color of the black 1969.

To back up the sales history of the silver car prior to restoration, another Ram Air IV four-speed 1970 version sold in 2005. Also essentially a basket case waiting for restoration, it was a red car that reportedly sold in excess of $300,000. Add to this the expense of a proper restoration using original parts, and we can establish that more than one person feels a Ram Air IV Judge convertible is worth investing roughly $500,000.

Pontiac affixed a small "Judge" graphic on the glove box door in case passengers forgot what was plastering them into the seats.

Remember Super Premium gasoline? Remember the sharp smell wafting around the rear of the car while the attendant filled the tank? The Muncie 4-speed manual really seemed to encourage anti-social behavior.

Mounting a rear wing on the trunk lid gave the Judge the visual drama lacking in the non-performance Pontiacs. It probably didn't generate much in the way of downforce, but it helped give the GTO the visual punch so necessary in street encounters.

Looking out over the long hood with a brawny V-8 burbling beneath your foot is one of the benefits of piloting a muscle car. Driving one today miraculously erases the years and will make anybody feel like a kid again.

A point worth mentioning regarding all Ram Air IV cars is their propensity to eat their own motors. In another "why did they do that?" move, Pontiac built the Ram Air IV motors with great free-flowing heads, a high-rpm valvetrain, a four-bolt main block with forged pistons, but swung them around with an Arma Steel crank and cast-iron connecting rods. Many Ram Air IV cars lost their original engine blocks very early on for this simple fact. Had the engines been built with forged connecting rods and a better crank, it may have been a different story, but as it is, don't expect to find many Ram Air IV cars with their original motor. Even though peak horsepower arrived at 5,500 rpm, these were a much better breathing engine than the non-round-port motors most buyers were used to. Couple this weakness with standard 3.90 or optional 4.33 gearing and a hot shoe behind the wheel, and you have an engine not capable of a lot of rpm getting wound tighter than a 300-pound coil spring. "Boom" is a good keyword here.

By 1971, the Ram Air IV engine was gone and the 17 1971 Judge convertibles produced were fitted with the new 455-ci HO round-port engine as standard equipment. These were lower compression motors, as were all 1971 GM powerplants. Basically, the 455 HO Ram Air engine fitted to the Judge was a four-bolt main block with cast pistons, a nodular iron crankshaft, Arma Steel connecting rods, Ram Air IV style round-port cylinder heads, a two-piece aluminum Ram Air IV style intake manifold, and special components such as a tuned Quadrajet and distributor. With a rated maximum horsepower of 335 at 4,800 rpm and a 5,200 rpm redline, these were deceptively powerful engines. The added 55 ci really paid huge dividends in the torque department, where Pontiac engines excelled.

If you drive a Ram Air IV and then hop into a 455 HO, the seat-of-the-pants feel will tell you the 455 HO is a far more usable motor. It is a relaxed yet powerful engine very well suited for a heavy

Pontiac built just 17 ragtop GTO Judges in 1971, making these some of the rarest muscle cars ever created. Because engines had continued to grow, so did the body.

In 1971 Ram Air on the hood still meant fresh air directed via functional hood scoops to the air cleaner.

car like a Judge convertible. In 1971, three Judge convertibles came with four-speed transmissions, and 14 with automatics. Values for a good 1971 Judge convertible were roughly $75,000–$100,000 in 2002–2003, and went to approximately $250,000–$300,000 by 2005. Today, I would peg a good four-speed version at $350,000–$400,000, and an automatic at $250,000–$300,000. They are a unique and equally rare alternative to the earlier Ram Air IV cars.

Bottom line? Any round-port GTO Judge convertible is at the top of the Pontiac pecking order. In my opinion, they are easily the equal of a Chevelle LS6 convertible, if not even more desirable. Why? A few reasons. First and foremost, there is factory documentation to document the cars and verify a real example. This is a huge benefit over an LS6; without original paperwork such as a build sheet, there is really no way to definitively prove an LS6 is real.

Almost as important is the fact that we know just how many round-port Judge convertibles were produced, with the exception of the 1970 model year. Even so, we do know there are far less than 37 1970 cars, and that is carved in stone. Second, the Judge convertible is very similar to cars like the Hemi 'Cuda convertibles in that it has exciting graphics and a definite image. Love it or hate it, there is nothing that looks quite like a Judge with loud stripes, bright colors, and a name based on a skit from the television show, *Laugh-In*. In the muscle car world, is there much more than the best engine of any given manufacturer, in its signature convertible, with ultra-low production numbers and factory paperwork available? Although they are not quite million-dollar muscle cars (yet), the round-port Judge convertibles are very deserving of their spot among the muscle car elite. ∎

166 ■ CHAPTER FOURTEEN

Pontiac fitted reflective decals over each wheel arch in an effort to give the Judge the visual flash to match the underhood thunder.

Right: The hood-mounted tach was a good idea that over time yellowed to unreadability. More a marketing tool than a useful feature, the design was uniquely Pontiac

Better living through cubic inches. Engines this size don't typically live for high rpm's, but they delivered more torque than the driveline knew what to do with.

Right: Pontiac ensured that a familial look wove through its entire product line, especially the twin-oval grille.

As muscle cars became more expensive, more affluent buyers were pursued, wooed by increasingly plush interiors. Pontiacs never lacked in creature comforts, and in 1971, the trend toward rolling hedonism continued.

Left: As emission regulations started to seep into Detroit, it was clear that the days of the monster-engined muscle car were fading. Yet Pontiac was determined to go out with a bang.

More for show than go, the dramatic rear spoiler did little to provide usable downforce, but it made a great place to mount the engine call-outs.

Left: General Motors' A-body platform spawned a goodly number of dramatic muscle cars, but few had the visual punch that the "Judge" did.

CHAPTER FIFTEEN

1970 CHEVROLET CHEVELLE SS 454 LS6 CONVERTIBLE

For the 1970 model year, GM lifted the corporate ban on any engine over 400 ci in its intermediate cars. In other words, the gloves were off and GM was ready to win the muscle car race. Prior to 1970, the only way to get a Chevelle with anything bigger than the 396-ci big block was through the fleet services department through the Central Office Production Order (COPO) program. Starting in 1970, though, you could order a 454-powered Super Sport Chevelle, a fact not lost on muscle car buyers. The top SS 454 engine was the new regular production order (RPO) code LS6. The LS6 has the highest-rated horsepower of any muscle car engine produced during the classic muscle-car era—450 horsepower, to be exact. With an incredible 500-plus lb-ft of torque, this was one hell of an engine. The specs read like a drag racer's dream: 11.25:1 compression ratio, big solid-lifter camshaft, huge Holley 780 CFM carburetor, 2.19-inch intake and 1.88-inch exhaust valves, aluminum intake manifold, four-bolt crankshaft main caps, and the list goes on. These were tough, strong motors and would easily give anything else on the street a run for its money. All told, 4,475 buyers checked the right box and had an SS 454 LS6 Chevelle built just for them.

Out of these 4,475 LS6 Chevelles built in 1970, approximately 20 to 25 of them were convertibles. The exact production figures may never be known, as Chevrolet has

Previous page, main: Not an often-ordered car, the LS-6 ragtop was the best of all worlds—fresh air, warm sun, and brutal power.

Previous page, inset: Though it looked similar to other big-block engines, the LS6's strong points were hidden from view. With a forged steel crankshaft and forged aluminum pistons, an aggressive solid lifter camshaft, and 11.25:1 compression, it was essentially a race engine in a street car.

A huge engine needs a huge carburetor. On the LS6, that would be a Holley #4492 800-cfm four-barrel. Mileage wasn't a concern.

An intermediate platform with a huge engine: a simple recipe for muscle car success. Handsome proportions and stylish wheels turned heads, while the monster engine could fry the tires without breaking a sweat.

not released the numbers nor admitted to even having them. For years, the generally accepted production number was 17 cars, and in recent years it has been bumped up to 21 cars. Whatever the exact number may be, it is certainly miniscule, and owning a documented LS6 convertible gives you membership into a very exclusive club. These are without question the Chevrolet equivalent of a Hemi 'Cuda convertible, and right at the top of anybody's dream list of legendary muscle cars. An SS 454 LS6 is a great driving car, with tons of power and styling that is immediately recognizable and still looks good today. For many, this is it, the car that was the high point of the entire muscle car era. After all, how many convertible muscle cars were capable of ripping off consistent mid-13-second quarter-mile times at over 100 miles per hour right out of the box?

Featured here is a fantastic 1970 LS6 Chevelle convertible. This screaming red M-22 Rock Crusher–equipped, 4.10:1 geared example is the way a street racer who liked a good suntan would have ordered it. No power options, a bench seat, and 450 horsepower with a stick coming up through the floor to grab gears with bright, loud, in-your-face LS6 attitude. It is owned by a collector in Indiana.

Like most ultradesirable, low-production muscle cars, 1970 LS6 convertible values have increased significantly in the last decade. One very well-known example, an M-22 four-speed-equipped car, was purchased from its original owner in 1989 for $130,000, a record price at the time. Later treated to a full restoration, it was sold again to a well-known collector for $140,000 in late

Only one manual transmission was available behind an LS6, the Muncie M-22. Although not silent in its work, it was virtually indestructible, a handy trait when funneling 450-plus horsepower.

Left: To think that anyone could walk into a Chevrolet dealership in 1970 and drive out in an LS6 Chevelle convertible is proof that America is a great country.

2001. Offered at the Barrett-Jackson auction on January 19, 2002, this same car stunned a lot of people when it brought another record price of $172,800. This car now resides in a private collection in Nevada, and its current owner values it at over $1 million.

The 2002 sale of this car was viewed as a fluke, or auction fever, at the time. Shortly after, however, the market spoke and this was the new level for LS6 convertibles. In November 2002, another four-speed LS6 convertible was sold at Mecum Auctions for $151,525, solidifying the six-figure values. As muscle car prices in general increased rapidly, ultra-rare cars such as LS6 convertibles kept pace and remained in front of the pack. By 2006, another LS6 sold for $513,000 at Barrett-Jackson, followed by the record sale of the Ray Allen/Briggs Chevrolet LS6 convertible drag car that sold, also at Barrett-Jackson in 2006, for $1,242,000. While the Ray Allen car was clearly an exception due to its history, any LS6 convertible documented as real is now worth over a half million dollars.

But let's discuss a key point in determining LS6 convertible values: documentation. This is the one area that really hurts Chevrolet muscle cars. Unlike a Chrysler product that has the original engine size encoded in the VIN, along with a fender tag that shows the entire original build configuration and all options, Chevrolet did not do this. Its serial numbers simply denoted whether a car was built as a six-cylinder or an eight-cylinder. Unlike Fords, Shelbys, or Buicks, there is no factory paperwork available to document the cars. There are not even published production numbers that can tell

With a spacious interior, it was possible to bring along friends and family while spanking other muscle cars at stoplights. Around town, the LS6 was not a highly strung beast, but floor the accelerator and all hell—and the rear tires—would break loose.

These tires were the best available in 1970, yet they didn't stand a chance against an LS6's torque. When cold, they tended to flat spot, making for an uncomfortable ride until the tire warmed up and assumed a circular shape.

us exactly how many of any particular model or engine combination were sold. All of this adds up to prime opportunity for dishonest people to make cars like an LS6 convertible out of thin air.

This, in turn, has kept values down and rightfully scares potential buyers. Like any collectible, provenance and known history are key, especially in cases such as LS6 cars, where one can be a complete fabrication. Build sheets, Protect-O-Plates, engine stampings, and date codes are great but easily forged. When it comes down to it, buyers want to know that what they are buying is the real deal, especially at these prices. So even though Chevy made fewer LS6 convertibles than Mopar did with its Hemi E Body convertibles, the key reason an LS6 is worth considerably less is this lack of absolute certainty. If Chevrolet would have encoded the serial numbers with an engine code, or released a definitive list of all LS6 convertible serial numbers, the values would be significantly stronger than what they are now. That being said, there is no denying a real LS6 convertible is the King Kong of the Chevelle world. One drive and you'll know what all the fuss is about. ■

Designed in an era when General Motors couldn't design a bad-looking car, the 1970 Chevelle LS6 was the high watermark for GM performance. Skyrocketing insurance rates doomed the car to dark garages.

Left: Prior to federally mandated bumper regulations, vehicle bumpers were pretty much just a stylistic element. They didn't have to be aerodynamic, so long as they looked good.

1970 CHEVROLET CHEVELLE SS 454 LS6 CONVERTIBLE

APPENDIX A:

ALTERNATIVES TO MILLION-DOLLAR MUSCLE

OK, so you've made it this far in the book and you are shaking your head saying, "Who the hell wants a car with a price that is as long as a damned phone number?" You love the cars, you appreciate them, and you understand what all the fuss is about. You want a rare muscle car with all the style and performance of the two-comma stuff, but you didn't just hit the lotto jackpot, or maybe your little brother the stock broker really didn't give you the "tip of a lifetime" on that WorldCom stuff. So you are looking for the best of both worlds, something rare and desirable, yet also something you can drive and have fun with. And you don't want to write all those damn zeros on the check. I can't say I blame you one bit. Let's look at some alternatives to million-dollar muscle that, in the real world, will be just as much fun to own and a little easier on the pocketbook.

The key to finding value in the muscle car market is to look for sleepers. These are cars that have all of the qualities of the ultra-rare stuff, but were either built in larger numbers, were built a little

Only 1,304 4-4-2 convertibles were built in 1971, and of those, just 110 featured the desirable W-30 option. Just 78 cars were fitted with the TH400 automatic, and very few of those were equipped with factory air conditioning as this car is. Part of the $369 W-30 package was a 455-ci blueprinted engine, along with specific drivetrain and chassis upgrades. It was truly an iron first in a silk glove.

before or a little after their holy grail stablemates, or haven't been discovered yet. What you are really looking for is a low-production car with the right ingredients, the right provenance, and the right quality. If you don't need to be the guy with a ZL1 Camaro at the local cruise night that had to trailer it in and can't leave the car alone for fear of somebody breathing on it, this is your chapter. Let's rattle through a few examples.

Instead of a ZL1 Camaro, find the best 1969 COPO 9561 427 Camaro you can with the cast-iron 425-horsepower L-72 engine. While it isn't a ZL1, it is 90 percent of the same thing for about 25 percent of the price. Exact production numbers are not known, but around 200 of these COPO units were shipped to Yenko Chevrolet and made into Yenko Camaros. If you want yours to say Yenko on it, just add another $100,000 or so onto the non-Yenko COPO price. You're still way under a ZL1, and you get some fancy stripes and wheels out of the deal, plus a nice bright orange engine rather than an as-cast aluminum one.

For alternatives to race cars such as the 1965 Shelby GT350 R Models, or even the 1965–1966 GT350 Drag Units, look at the street version of the car they are based on. In the case of the 1965 GT350, instead of an R Model (one of 36), a no-brainer alternative is buying a one-of-521 production 1965 street GT350s. The best one you can find will be less than half of an R Model, and you can drive it on the street and enjoy the car. It's essentially the same vehicle, the only difference being the street car is trimmed out with a full interior, mufflers, and other street equipment. The chassis and brakes are almost identical, as is the driving experience. I am a big fan of 1965 GT350 street cars and drive the wheels off of mine every chance I get. Don't get me wrong, I love the R Models and they are hugely significant to the Shelby legend. But if I had to pick between the street and competition version, I'd put a street car in my garage as it is far more usable. After all, if you can't drive them, what is the point?

In the Mopar world, Hemi cars aren't the only low-production cars worth paying attention to. If you want a wing car like the 1969 Charger Daytona Hemi featured here, but don't want to pay the freight on one of those babies, how about a 440-ci, 375-horsepower Daytona? It's still an ultra-rare car with all the looks of the Hemi and has one less carburetor to mess with. They are about half the price of a good Hemi Daytona. Or try a 1970 Plymouth Superbird if you just have to have a place to hang your laundry but don't want to step up to Daytona money. A 440-ci, 375-horsepower Superbird will run around $125,000, and for a 'Bird that will give a Hemi Daytona a run for its money, try a 440 Six Pack Superbird, which has 390 horsepower and, just like my diet, a lot of carbs. While it isn't a Hemi, a 440 Six Pack with its triple Holley carbs has a ton of curb appeal and it runs like a freight train. E-Bodies? There are some really rare, low-production number 'Cuda and Challenger convertibles not equipped

As one of General Motors top divisions, Oldsmobile had a reputation for upscale interior appointments, and this level of comfort wasn't compromised in the 4-4-2 W-30. Buyers could choose between a Hurst shifted 4-speed manual or a Hurst Dual-Gate equipped TH400 3-speed automatic.

Top, left: Bearing an aggressive yet stylish prow, the 4-4-2 was the most upscale General Motors A-body to enjoy attention from the performance engineers.

ALTERNATIVES TO MILLION-DOLLAR MUSCLE ■ 179

Oldsmobile called the W-30 blueprinted engine, which featured an aluminum intake manifold and a hot camshaft, "Select-Fit."

Top, right: Contrasting stripes on the fiberglass functional hood scoops denoted a 4-4-2, and the bright red front inner fenders meant it was a W-30. This was the Oldsmobile performance car for 1971.

Compression dropped in 1971, yet 350 horsepower and 460 lb-ft of torque was still enough to get in trouble.

with Hemis and also don't have the price tag today that the Hemis do. I've owned a bunch of 383 and 440 E Body convertibles, and they are just as much fun as a Hemi car. My favorite was a Sublime-over-white 383 Challenger R/T that was loaded with options including factory air conditioning. I sold it for less than the sales tax on a Hemi Challenger convertible.

Love the 1969 Trans Am convertibles featured in this book? Again, for about 10 percent of what one of those will cost *if* one ever comes up for sale, you can have one of 689 RAIII Trans Am hardtops produced in 1969. Think of the money you'll save on sunblock alone!

If you lust after a Ram Air IV Judge convertible, a great bang-for-the-buck alternative to these double-digit production cars is available and is so similar that the only external difference is a Roman numeral "III" on the hood scoops. It is the Ram Air III Judge convertible. While you can't count them on one hand, they are still among the top collectible Pontiac muscle cars of all time, with just 108 produced in 1969 and 168 produced in 1970. The good news is that a Ram Air III Judge convertible can still be found for less than half of what a Ram Air IV version would cost. And you'll

Though Buick quietly pursued performance during the classic Muscle Car era, it did it with typical Buick style—not overly flashy, but comfortable and highly effective at building velocity.

likely have the only one at any show you attend outside of the GTO Owner's Association national convention. In the real world, I doubt you'd ever notice or need the additional horsepower offered by the Ram Air IV over the Ram Air III. Even under the hood the cars look very similar, with a few differences only astute GTO aficionados will notice. It is certainly not like the difference between a 383 four-barrel 'Cuda versus a 426 dual quad Hemi 'Cuda with a Shaker hood. As proof of how much I feel the real value in Judge convertibles is with the Ram Air III version, I own a 1969 four-speed car. I've had lots of Ram Air IV cars, and for the difference in the cost of admission, I'll take a Ram Air III car with a nice Ram Air IV Judge hardtop to park next to it for the same money—and still have plenty of gas money left!

For other GM A Body alternatives, how about finding one for the Chevelle LS6 convertible? Well, the obvious choice is another Chevelle droptop with a lower horsepower motor, such as an LS5 or even a really rare L78 396/375 horsepower version. But if you want to get something a little more exclusive than a big-block Chevelle convertible that looks like one of the 10 SS clones that seems to be at every show, how about looking at other GM cars? With performance on par with the mighty LS6, a Buick GS Stage 1 convertible is a really good choice. With a 455-ci ram air engine that lays down 510 lb-ft of torque stock, the most of any classic muscle car, and a really well-developed chassis that has ride and handling qualities second to none, these are great cars. Just 232 Stage 1 GS convertibles were produced in 1970, and only 81 in 1971. These cars have been real sleepers for a long time and people are just starting to figure it out. Get one while you can; they are under $200,000 now, but I don't think they will be there for long.

Not a Buick person? How about one of Dr. Oldsmobile's best creations: the 1970–1971 442 W30 convertible? With looks more along the lines of the LS6 Chevelle, the W30 convertible has even a little more flash. A very aggressive fiberglass ram air hood, covered in stripes, plus stripes and special badges down the side of the car, really set a W Machine off. Add to this the W30 (and Oldsmobile)

ALTERNATIVES TO MILLION-DOLLAR MUSCLE   181

For years, "When better automobiles are built, Buick will build them" was the company slogan, and when examining a 1970 Stage 1 GS 455, it's clear the division practiced what it preached.

Bottom, left: It took a keen eye to catch the Stage 1 emblem on the fender of a GS. Buick wasn't a division prone toward gaudy callouts.

Bottom, right: Leave it to Buick to create a honking muscle car engine that looked tasteful while being able to destroy rear tires with ease. The Stage 1 GS 455 covered the quarter-mile in 13.79 seconds at 104.5 seconds for *Motor Trend* magazine. These engines produced 510 lb-ft of torque, and torque is what gets the job done.

exclusive bright red front inner fenders, and these are great-looking cars. While the W30 455-ci ram air engine may not have had the raw power of Chevy's 454 LS6, the Olds was no slouch. These cars had lots of great performance-minded options available, such as a W27 cast-aluminum rear differential. Just 264 W30 convertibles were built in 1970, and rarer still are the 1971 W30 convertibles with only 110 produced. While both the Buick GS Stage 1 and Oldsmobile 442 W30 may not have been as rare, as lean, or as mean as the Chevelle SS 454 LS6, they are still super-rare and fantastic cars to live with. For a lot less money.

Again, I will put my money where my mouth is and tell you that I own the 1971 442 W30 convertible pictured on these pages. To show that super-rare cars are still out there waiting to be discovered, I found this W30 advertised, of all places, on eBay. It had been owned by a small-town grade-school teacher in Iowa since 1972. It was her everyday, year-round car. She drove it to work and shuttled her now grown sons around in it for many years. A few years ago, a friend of hers heard that muscle cars were getting popular and encouraged her to park the W30 because it could be worth "over ten thousand dollars someday." This same friend, years later, took the W30 out of storage and advertised it on eBay. It was in very tired but very original condition, well worth saving. I purchased the car in 2006, and muscle car experts Karl Kreis and Mark Klos have recently completed a ground-up restoration on it. Because it

Rather rare, only 232 Buicks were ordered in such an aggressive package. Being a midsize platform, the trunk was large enough to hold the folded convertible top comfortably, giving the GS a sleek look.

was an Oldsmobile, and looked horrible with the original top duct-taped together and 20-plus-year-old Town and Country snow tires on it, I was able to buy this car as a diamond in the rough for far less than an LS6 convertible in the same shape would have cost. Now completely restored to new condition, it is a no-questions car with great history and paperwork, and one of 110 produced. If you ever get tired of looking for the proverbial barn-find muscle car, just remember that your next great purchase may be closer than you think. Heck, it might even be on eBay. I can hear the stampede heading for every small-town school teacher right now.

The best advice I can give for finding a great alternative to your dream million-dollar muscle car is to be creative. Look at similar cars from the same manufacturer, but also keep it limited to rare, low-production cars. Then hunt down the best one you can find. Think about what you are going to use the car for, and pick accordingly. I like driving my cars, and I like having unique low-production examples. Most of the owners of the million-dollar examples earlier in the book don't exercise them for obvious reasons. But quite a few have very similar alternatives that they do use. After all, if you are a car nut, you aren't happy just looking at your cars. So plug away on Google, crack open those old, dusty production-number books, scan the classified ads and eBay, and poke around at car shows and cruise nights. Before you know it, you'll find an alternative to million-dollar muscle that suits you and your budget. ■

Bottom, left: In a Buick, it's assumed that superior interior appointments will cosset occupants, and the Stage 1 GS 455 didn't stray from that assumption. Better-quality materials and close attention to fit and finish made driving, and riding in, the muscular Buick a treat.

Bottom, right: Functional hood scoops on a Buick? The normally staid division broke new Buick design ground when the GS wore twin nostrils. But in typical Buick fashion, they were discreet and tasteful.

ALTERNATIVES TO MILLION-DOLLAR MUSCLE

APPENDIX B:
A REAL-WORLD BUYER'S GUIDE

Whether you are going to spend $5,000 or $5 million on a muscle car, it does not make sense to be spending your money foolishly. After all, money isn't easy to come by, and as our parents used to tell us, it doesn't grow on trees (at least not in my yard). This is the part of the book that hopefully will benefit anybody looking at any kind of collectible car. One might think that, as a collector car dealer, I would try to protect our time-honored traditions of sawdust in noisy differentials and oatmeal in leaky radiators. Not so. I've been buying and selling cars since I was 13 years old, and I have learned a few things that I'd like to share.

Let's face facts: The collector car world is filled with fraud, deception, games, and downright crooks, just as in any other industry. It used to be a minor issue when muscle cars traded for $5,000 to $10,000; the incentive for forgers and dishonest people was very low and the downside for buyers was minimal. If you bought an LS-6 Chevelle for $7,500 and it turned out to be a $3,000 Malibu, well, shame on you and on to the next car. You learned your lesson (hopefully) and most likely now knew how to spot a real LS-6 versus a fake one. Nobody lost everything over a car deal.

Ford data plates, located at the rear edge of the driver's door, are a wealth of information. They contain everything from the day the car was born, to where it was shipped, to the original color, axle ratio, and transmission. This Boss 429 also has its Kar Kraft sequential production number on the decal above the data plate. These are original tags; use caution when shopping because very convincing forged tags are commonplace.

Today, the risk is far more severe. Let's say you buy a $600,000 LS-6 Convertible that later proves to be a forgery. You now have a very substantial financial wound, and a $75,000 (at best) clone car to remind you of it. This is an extreme example. Fraud and deception more commonly revolve around cars that have their condition misrepresented, bogus paperwork, or non-original components disguised as original. The more valuable cars become, the more rewarding it is for unscrupulous folks to deceive buyers, which leads to higher levels of sophistication and dishonesty. Technology has also made it far easier to create everything from "original" window stickers and build sheets on laser printers to new vehicle identification numbers (VIN) and cowl tags.

So how do muscle car enthusiasts looking to buy a car protect themselves from sellers whose goal is to prey on them? Simple: use the following steps to determine just what you are looking at and who you are buying it from.

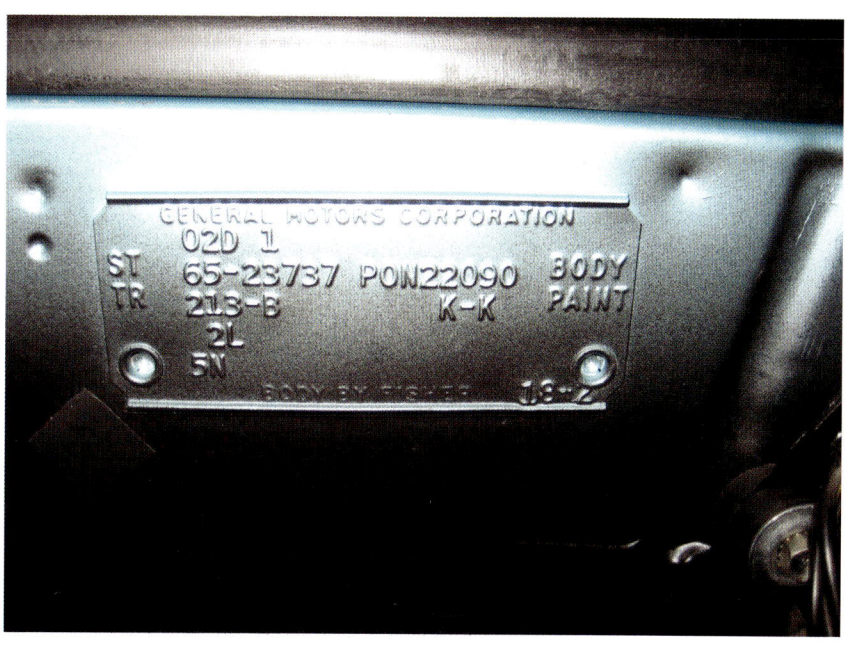

A GTO birth certificate. While not as conclusive as a Mopar or Ford data plate, GM cowl tags narrow things down. They contain the build date for the body, which can then be compared to the casting dates of all major components on the car. Remember, the chicken came before the egg.

Rule Number One: Buy What You Like

The first rule is to narrow your search and decide just what kind of car you want. If you are a Ford guy, don't decide to look at Chevrolets because you saw a few that were great deals. Buying a car purely for financial gain is a great way to take the passion out of any experience. Buy what you truly love, and buy it for the enjoyment the car itself will offer. You cannot put a price on finally getting the Boss 302 you have always wanted and getting to drive it whenever you want. The emotional rewards should be just as important as the financial ones, so buying what you like should be your first priority. Obviously, the investment aspect is important as well, but if you want something that isn't exciting and guarantees a return, I hear savings bonds are still being printed.

Rule Number Two: Get Smart

Once you've decided what type of car you are after, become the newest authority on the subject. Even if you just narrow it down to a particular genre, say, Trans-Am race cars, read everything you can get your hands on about them. Study all of the Trans-Am cars: the Boss 302s, Mopar AAR 'Cudas and Trans-Am Challengers, Z/28 Camaros, and AMC Javelins. Sometimes just reading about the general style of car will make it easy to decide which one is your favorite. One of the greatest tools at your disposal is the Internet. With a few clicks, you can be off and running with a Google search about the car of your dreams. The amount of information available to us today is staggering, and much of it wasn't around even 10 years ago. Use it. Ask questions of the experts, join the owners' club, chime in and ask questions on Internet club forums. Go to shows, especially national conventions, where concours judging takes place and numerous examples of good cars abound. For the price of a hot dog or a few beers, a concours judge or knowledgeable club member might let you tag along during judging.

Ask to see judging sheets and learn just what is important on the particular model you desire. For example, a 1969 four-speed Pontiac GTO with a Ram Air engine has a special carburetor. If it is missing (and most are), you'd be lucky to find one for less than $3,000. Every car has unique little details like this. Learn the basics: where the spot welds should be on body panels, where the date codes and serial numbers should be on the engine and transmission, how to verify key components, and how to decode trim tags and paperwork. You will not learn everything there is to know, but if you arm yourself with a general overview of what to look for, you will be much better off. Sometimes a day spent on the show field or a $25 book on the subject is worth its weight in gold.

Rule Number Three: Listen to What the Car Is Telling You
After learning the basics of what to look for on the car itself, move on to the basics of documenting the car at hand. Original paperwork and documentation is key. I will not buy a car without verifiable original documentation and neither should you.

There are a few exceptions, however. The 1961 and newer Pontiacs can be verified through Pontiac Historic Services, which has the original GM billing history for nearly every vintage Pontiac. The Shelby American Automobile Club (SAAC) has similar records for Shelby Cobras and Mustangs, and takes documentation one step further. The SAAC publishes the Shelby American World Registry, which not only lists every Shelby ever made, but also the known history of each particular car. This is an invaluable resource and indisputedly the definitive go-to book for anybody considering a Shelby. Fords built in 1967 or later have documentation available through Marti Auto Works, which has the original Ford production records. Buick buyers can obtain documentation from the Sloan Museum and the GS historical society.

Beyond original paperwork or documentation from one of these sources that has production information available, one must verify the actual history of the car. This is the most daunting and tedious task of all. The only way to really know where a car has been is to talk to past owners or anybody else who may know the car. Sometimes the current owner will have this information already, or you will be lucky and find a car from the original owner. If not, making some calls to the Department of Motor Vehicles in every state in which you know the car has been titled and doing basic detective work will usually turn up previous owners. Once you get one, the owner will usually lead you to the person he or she bought the car from, and perhaps even the person he or she sold the car to. Again, it is a tedious and time-consuming task, but very worthwhile for anybody considering a high-dollar purchase.

Even the most seemingly insignificant components can be very important. Here, a Rally II wheel from a 1969 Pontiac Judge Convertible tells us its life story. Both the date built and original application info are stamped into the rim. As most muscle cars quickly lost their original wheels, finding a car with its original shoes is a real bonus. If missing, these can be expensive items needed to make a car truly "numbers matching."

Rule Number Four: Know What It's Really Worth
Now that you know what to look for, it is time to determine market value. Knowing the right questions to ask (does your 1969 GTO Ram Air car have the original 273 carb?) will help you separate the good cars from the bad ones reasonably quickly. Browse *Hemmings Motor News*, the Internet, eBay, and private party and dealer ads, and track asking prices. If a car looks too cheap, it probably isn't. Ask your new best friends in the owners' clubs and talk forums what they think the car you want should be worth. Usually the guys that own a particular car keep track of market value, similar to a homeowner watching asking prices on homes in their neighborhood.

And if you are expecting a big lecture on how you should only buy a car from a dealer because I am one, well, don't hold your breath. I look at and buy hundreds of cars a year, and I can tell you

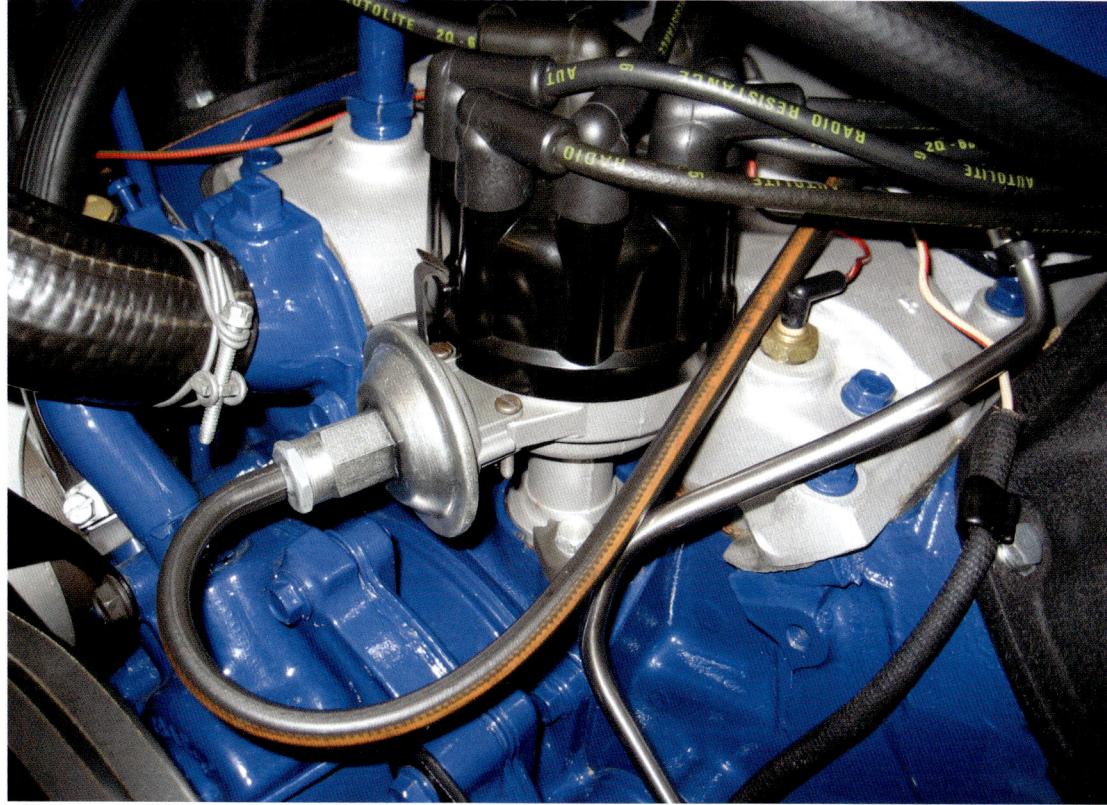

This 1969 Shelby GT-350 engine is awfully pretty. Looking beyond the shine, proper research will tell you if it is correct. Don't let great detail work draw your eye away from hidden sins.

from experience that there are really good dealers, and really bad ones. Same can be said of private-party sellers or anybody else selling something, from an outboard boat motor to an airplane: for some reason, even the most honest people can become anything but honest when the almighty dollar is involved. I've bought great cars from people I know to be flat-out thieves, and I've bought absolute junk cars from people I thought walked on water. Just remember, every deal is a new one and every car is a new case study.

Good cars are hard to find, so if you see one that really strikes your fancy and the initial gut-check scratch-and-sniff test says you should look into it, don't let who is selling it scare you away. The most important lesson is to always, without exception, buy the best example you can. I know it sounds simple, but you would be amazed at the false economy people talk themselves into. You cannot make a silk purse out of a sow's ear. Using the Boss 302 example, the worst example out there will cost a minimum of $20,000, without a motor, transmission, or any Boss-specific parts that now cost a fortune. A proper restoration to concours level with parts will be $125,000 or more at any professional shop. You would then have $145,000 or more in a car that is worth around $100,000, three years down the road and many headaches later. So even if you only have $20,000 to spend, use it as a down payment, go and buy the best Boss 302 you can for $100,000, and finance the balance if you have to.

The other important consideration in buying the best is not only condition, but also provenance. A truly unique car with special history, such as an original unrestored car, a one-owner car, a special color not offered as a regular production option, or a wealth of original paperwork is worth far more to me than an average example of the same car. How much more it will be worth is up to you, the buyer, and every car is different. I can tell you that the cars in my personal collection were all chosen because they are special, be it original paint, rare options, or one-off examples. I paid a premium for all of them and still consider it the best money I have ever spent.

Original paperwork such as a legitimate window sticker is worth its weight in gold. This Boss 429 sticker is the real deal, but only a highly trained eye can detect the few differences that differentiate it from masterfully forged duplicates. With the advent of laser printers and high-tech techniques to add "patina," if in doubt, it's best to have an expert examine the documentation. In extreme instances firms exist that can literally test the paper and tell you how old (or new) it is. As the bad guys hone their skills so must the good guys.

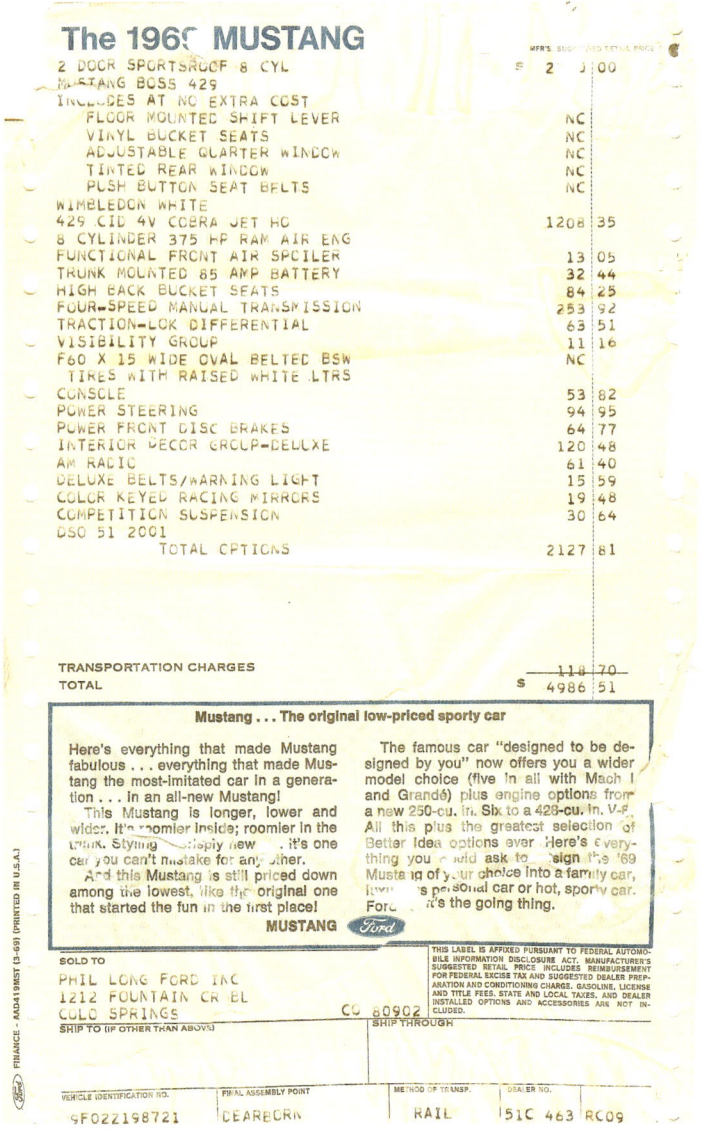

Next, it is time to meet your blind date. To paraphrase the recent MasterCard commercials: Plane ticket: $500; hotel room: $100; collector car: $75,000; knowing what you are really buying: priceless. What am I telling you? Don't ever buy a car sight unseen from somebody you do not know. Period. If Las Vegas offered $1,000 bets where you could potentially lose $100,000, how many people do you think would take them? That is the risk-versus-reward bet you are taking by not hopping on a plane and looking at the car you are considering.

Don't think you are sharp enough to verify numbers and condition? Hire an expert. It is money well spent, especially if it saves you from making a mistake and buying the wrong car. Planning on shopping at an auction? Call the auction company ahead of time, and see if you can get any additional information on the car or owner. If a consignment contract is in place, most auction houses won't mind you speaking with the consignor. If nothing else, get the VIN or copies of any paperwork the auction may have on file and take as much due diligence as you can before auction day. The good news about auctions is that usually the experts for any number of makes will be attending the bigger sales and can be hired to do on-site inspections.

Once you see the car and are pleased with it, the documentation, and your research so far, it is time to do the interview. Are you dealing with the owner, or a broker? Whenever possible, try to get directly to the owner. Ask the tough questions, and note how the seller responds. Just like a police interrogation, ask the same questions two or three times, but phrased differently. See if the answers match. Don't accept "numbers matching" as being the original engine. Clearly ask if it is the original, factory-installed, numbers-matching engine for this car. Ask if the car needs anything and if everything works. Ask a simple question such as, "If you were to keep the car, is there anything you would do to it?"

Most importantly, even though you are hammering away with tough questions, be respectful and polite. I know it sounds simple, but a seller who feels he or she is being treated fairly will always respond better and usually with the same respect for you. When I am selling a car, I put myself in the buyer's shoes and look at it from the buyer's perspective. I also feel strongly that unless the seller gives you reason to, don't put basic courtesy aside. After all, the seller is likely a car person just like you are. I've been involved in deals with rude sellers, and ones with rude buyers. The end result is always the same; the dander goes up and nothing gets accomplished.

If you are worried about a car being sold before you can do a proper pre-purchase inspection, show the seller you are sincere and offer a nonrefundable deposit to hold the car for a reasonable amount of time. Discuss inspection schedules and how final payment is to be made. No matter what, do not be pushed into buying a car that is not exactly the right car for you, that isn't as represented, and that doesn't have a clean history. Nothing stings more than knowing you bought a pig in a poke.

While not a definitive guide, hopefully this will help you keep the basics in mind for your next purchase. Decide what you like, study, verify if it is real, know who you are buying from, and rest easy knowing you did it the right way.

This 1969 Camaros original Protect-O-Plate and Owner's Manual are talking. Are you listening? The Protect-O-Plate is often the only definitive way to determine what you are really looking at. General Motors had to place the important info on these for warranty and parts identification when new. Everything from the engine code to the selling dealer and original owner's name is present. Just be careful; bogus P-O-P's have been getting stamped out for years. Original blanks and even the tape often show up on eBay.

INDEX

Adams, Herb, 80
Al Grillo Ford, 126
Alan Mann Racing Team, 32
Allen, Ray, 175
Aloha Dream Cars, 24
Ambassador Hotel, 112, 113
American Hot Rod Association (AHRA), 97
American Road Race of Champions (ARRC), 30
Anderson, Cal, 154, 155
Auto Motor Sport, 32
Autoweek, 64
Backhaus, William, 49
Baker, Buddy, 152
Baldwin Chevrolet, 131
Barnhart, Ken, 90, 92–94
Barrett-Jackson, 18, 123, 155, 175
Berger Chevrolet, 139
Berry Plastic Glass Company, 122
Braun, Hans, 33
Briggs Chevrolet, 175
Brown Brothers Ford, 35, 36
Budzinski, Gary, 49, 53
Buhl, Walter, 33
Burns, Mell, 123
Car and Driver magazine, 111
Car Craft magazine, 46, 47, 155
Chandler, Otis, 20, 93, 155
Chevrolet
  Camaro Sunoco, 69
  Camaro Z/28, 68–77, 81
  Camaro ZL1, 9, 72, 86–95, 139, 179
  Caprice, 20
  Chevelle SS 454 LS, 172–177, 181
  Corvette ZR-1, 73
  Engineering, 69
  LS6 Chevelle, 8
  Yenko 427 Nova, 138–147
Christenholz, Dave, 18, 20, 23, 24, 93, 94

Christie, Dave, 99, 100, 104, 105
Chrysler 300, 43
Classic Sixties magazine, 44
Cobra Automotive, 34, 36
Cohen, Larry, 114, 116
Conley, Craig, 34
Cote, Bob, 34
Creative Industries, 154
Dana Chevrolet, 139
Day, Dick, 46
DeLorean, John, 111
DiPasquale, Phil, 125
Dodge
  Challenger R/T Hemi, 23, 24, 26, 27
  Charger Daytona Hemi, 148–157, 179
  Dart GSS 440, 130–137
Donohue, Mark, 69
Drag Strip magazine, 64
Duesenberg SJ, 8, 9
Durham, Booth, 114
Eber, Ken, 36
Estes, Pete, 70–74, 81, 87
Ferrari 250 GTO, 111
Ferrari Testarossa, 8
Ferron, Jim, 125
Flannery, Pat, 47, 113
Fogg Motors Ltd., 35
Ford
  Advanced Vehicles (FAV), 32, 39
  Boss 429, 13
  Mercury Cyclone Spoiler, 150
  Mustang, 29, 30
  Shelby Cobra Dragonsnake, 121, 127
  Shelby Cobra Mustang, 30
  Shelby GT350, 28–41, 57, 79, 120–129
  Shelby GT350 R, 7, 8, 30–41, 179
  Shelby GT500 Super Snake, 56–67

  Torino Talladega, 150
Fuller Ford, 125
Funk, Kenn, 93
George May Ford, 123
Gibb, Fred, 87, 89, 90
Goodell, Fred, 62
Gorman, James, 65
Grand Spalding Dodge, 131–134, 137
Grappone, John, 125
Great Lakes Dragaway, 47, 55
Grillo, Al, 126
GTO Association of America (GTOAA), 53
Guarise, Mike, 105, 106
Gurney, Dan, 112, 113
Hadden, James, 65
Hamilton, Tommy, 35, 36, 39
Hammond, Gene, 32
Hemmings Motor News, 16, 17, 19, 114, 162, 186
Hesterman, Walter, 34
Highway Motors, 126
Hi-Performance Motors, Inc., 125, 126
Honolulu Auto Center, 123
Hot Rod magazine, 46, 47
Hudson Hornet, 43, 87
Hurst Performance Products, 43, 52, 112
Hurst, George, 43–47, 52, 54, 112–114, 116, 118, 119, 132, 135
International Hot Rod Association (IHRA), 97
Isaac, Bobby, 152, 157
J. W. Automotive, 32
Jenkins, Bill, 90, 92
Johnson, Don, 20, 23
Joseph, Greg, 20, 93
Kar Kraft, 184
Kennedy Chrysler-Plymouth, 19
King, Jake, 99, 100, 102
Klein, Dean, 104–106

Klos, Mark, 182
Kraus, Norm, 131–135
Kreis, Karl, 182
Krolick, Ron, 34
Lampone, Alex, 46, 47, 52
Landy, Dick, 104, 105
Liberty Performance, 105
Lillard, Charles, 65, 85
Lindberg, Erik, 105, 106
Lions Drag Strip, 123
Loedenberg, David, 65
Ludwig, Harry, 123
Mann, Alan, 32
Markley, Bill, 71
Marti Auto Works, 186
Martin, Buddy, 97, 99, 106
Mashall Motor Co., 126
Mattison, Jim, 52, 83, 114, 116, 139
May, George, 123
Maynard, Al, 74
McCain, Don, 64, 121–123
Mecum Collector Car Auction, 16, 17, 73, 83, 175
Mecum, Dana, 16, 17, 73–75
Mel Burns Ford, 64, 65, 123
Miles, Ken, 39
Milwaukee Journal, 47
Monteverde, Carlos, 18
Moore, Mitch, 144
Mopar Action, 17, 18
Motor Trend magazine, 79, 112, 113, 118, 119
Motorsport magazine, 36
Mustang Illustrated magazine, 123
Nash Bridges, 23
National Hot Rod Association (NHRA), 46, 47, 52, 97, 98, 100
Neerpasch, Jochen, 32, 39
New York Times, 18
Newhardt, David, 125
Nickey Chevrolet, 131
Nye, Vern, 73
Oberste Nationale Sportbehörde, 33
Pardee, Howard, 35, 36, 126, 127
Parks, Wally, 46, 52
Penske, Roger, 69
Performance Associates, 122, 123, 126, 127
Petersen Publishing, 43
Petersen, Robert, 113
Pfugfelder, Paul, 34
Pierce, Bobby, 65
Piggins, Vince, 69–71, 87
Pistol Grip shifter, 8
Plymouth
   Hemi 'Cuda, 7, 8, 13–27, 162, 166, 174
   Sox & Martin 'Cuda, 96–107
   Superbird, 152, 153, 155, 179
Pontiac
   Firebird Trans Am, 78–85, 180
   GTO, 29, 43–45
   GTO Judge Round-Port, 158–171, 180
   Historic Services, 52, 114
   Hurst GeeTO Tiger, 42–55, 111, 114
   Hurst Motor Trend Riverside "500" Pace Car, 52, 53, 110–119
   Super Duty, 8
   Tempest, 114
   Tin Indian, 111
Quam, Les, 125
Rallye Racing magazine, 33
Rand/Workman auction, 18
Rath, Martin, 33
Ritchey, Les, 122
Riverside Raceway, 112
Road and Track magazine, 79
Robson, Milton, 16, 17, 73, 74, 85, 162
Rogal, Peter, 36
Roush, William, 36
San Fernando Raceway, 123
Segal, Steve, 19
Shelby American Automobile Club (SAAC), 34–36, 122, 125, 127, 186
Shelby, Carroll, 29, 60, 62, 64, 140
Smith, Jeff, 36
Sox, Willard "Ronnie," 97, 99, 106
Sports Car Club of America (SCCA), 29, 30, 33, 69, 72, 77, 79, 80, 140
Standen, Thomas H., 72, 73
Steele, Bill, 32
Steele, Rich, 74
Stickman, Bill, 19
Stidwell, Mike, 36
Supercar Specialties, 74
Suydam, Devin, 20
Theissen, Friedhelm, 32
Tiemann, Scott, 74
Titus, Jerry, 30, 39, 81
Treleven, Jerry, 49, 52
Trusdale, Brian, 106
Urban, Jim, 49, 53
Urbaniak, Dennis, 47, 53
USA Today, 18
V. V. Cooke Chevrolet, 144
Virginia International Raceway, 34
Vogt, Curt, 34
von Wendt, Freiherr, 32, 35
Wadsworth, William, 126
Wangers, Jim, 43, 44, 49, 53, 112
Watertown Dodge, 154
Watson, Jack, 47
Watters, George, 36
Weimann, Bill, 18
Wellborn, Tim, 155
Whaling City Ford, 126
Whit Chevrolet, 92, 93, 95
Wood, Arden "Biff," 126
Wyer, John, 32, 39
Yeager, Tom, 31
Yeko, Pete, 47, 49, 53
Yenko Chevrolet, 139–141, 144, 145, 179
Yenko, Don, 87, 131, 132, 136, 140, 141, 143–145
Zazarine, Paul, 53, 116
Zuidema, Gus, 122

ACKNOWLEDGMENTS

This book would not be possible without the help given by the following people. Whether it was sharing information, a great car story, the loan of an irreplaceable muscle car, or simple encouragement, these are true friends to the collector car hobby: Cal Anderson; Ken Barnhart; Arnie "The Farmer" Beswick; Dave Christenholz; Tom Clary/Yenko Sportscar Club; Ken Funk; Mike Guarise; Reggie Jackson; Bill Jenkins; Greg Joseph; Ron Krolick; Charley Lillard; Bob Lutz; Keith Martin/*Sports Car Market Magazine*; Jim Mattison/Pontiac Historic Services; Al Maynard; Dana Mecum; Dan Pausch; Lester Quam; Phil Silva; Scott Tiemann/Supercar Specialties; Brett Torino; Dennis Urbaniak; Curt Vogt/Cobra Automotive; Jim Wangers; Bill Weimann; Pete Yeko; and a fellow who unfortunately comes last in any alphabetized list, but who is far from least, Paul Zazarine; as well as the many others who have graciously shared their passion for these unique cars. To all of you I offer my sincere thanks. I owe you more than just a few gallons of high-test and some Polyglas tread.

On a personal note, I do not consider myself a writer. When Darwin Holmstrom called me out of the blue to ask if I wanted to write this book, my knee-jerk reaction was "no." While honored by the offer, I was quite sure I was going to pass. Not wanting to seem impulsive, I explained that I would need to check my calendar and call him back. Truth be told, I decided to make three calls. Anything less than all three people agreeing I should write the book, I decided, would be a "no" for Darwin. So I called the three people I was sure would talk me out of it. Surprisingly, all three told me I had to write the book. I thought for a minute that maybe I should make three more calls and try to shoot for a tie. Obviously, since you are holding the book in your hands you know what I told Darwin the next day. I haven't regretted it for a second. Darwin, thanks for the call, and to my father Brendan Comer, Jennifer Bennett, and Alex Brunkhorst, thanks for answering. To the rest of my friends and family, thank you for tolerating my absence while I was locked to a computer keyboard. I couldn't have done it without you.

I couldn't have asked for better training wheels at MBI than Darwin Holmstrom and Zack Miller. These guys are the calm in the storm and made it all look easy. Thanks.

And finally, having automotive photographer extraordinaire David Newhardt bring the sizzle to this steak is an honor. David spent countless hours on the road traveling coast to coast to capture the images between these two covers. It took many early mornings, late nights, and rainy days camped in hotel rooms, but I think you'll agree it was worth it. Thanks, David!

Enjoy your stroll through some of the finest muscle cars ever. After that, go make some race gas flow through that Holley carb and bang that Hurst shifter through the gears. Isn't that what it's all about?

Colin Comer
Milwaukee, Wisconsin

As a twenty-year overnight success, I've worked with dozens of authors on scores of projects. Some books can be a struggle, while others are a labor of love. This book, with Colin Comer, strongly leans towards the latter category. While this is Colin's first book, he's no stranger to hammering out highly readable prose, delivering an insightful look at the muscle car world each month in the pages of *Sports Car Market*. This book is clear evidence that he shouldn't shy away from the keyboard.

Both of us love muscle cars, and I hope that love comes through in these words and images. Logistics can be a difficult hurdle to overcome when attempting to secure access to any vehicle, and the rarity of these could have made access an impossible task, since most of these cars are extremely rare, and in at least one instance, the only example in existence. But the owners of these vehicles went out of their way to make their cars camera ready, even when schedules, weather, or just bad luck could have prevented the shoot from ever happening. The words "thank you" don't seem adequate.

A number of individuals helped me bounce around the country like a professional tumbleweed, opening doors on short notice, helping me get the right location at the right time, usually on short notice. Richard and Elaine Bonnefoi make Chicago accessible and welcoming, while Michael Warren and Bill Taylor at Events Solution International helped to smooth many a bumpy road. Leonard and Patricia Cradit helped to keep me off the street while trying to get "just one more shot." The folks behind the scenes are invaluable, indispensable, and worth their weight in gold. Thank you all.

While Colin has thanked Darwin Holmstrom and Zack Miller, I must throw in my two cents. I've worked with this pair of professionals for ten years, and their patience and gentle guidance have helped to make my job one of the best in the world. Working with car people makes all the difference.

David Newhardt
Pasadena, California